THE INTERCESSORY LIFE

THE INTERCESSORY LIFE
Breaking the Impossibility Barrier

MAXIE D. DUNNAM

seedbed

Copyright 2013 by Maxie D. Dunnam

All rights reserved. No portion of this book may be reproduced, stored in a retrieval system, or transmitted in any form or by any means—electronic, mechanical, photocopy, recording, scanning, or other— except for brief quotations in critical reviews or articles, without the prior written permission of the publisher.

All scripture quotations, unless otherwise indicated, are taken from the Holy Bible, New International Version®, NIV®. Copyright © 1973, 1978, 1984, 2011 by Biblica, Inc.™ Used by permission of Zondervan. All rights reserved worldwide.

Scripture quotations marked ESV are taken from the Holy Bible: English Standard Version, copyright © 2001, Wheaton: Good News Publishers. Used by permission. All rights reserved.

Scripture quotations marked KJV are taken from the Holy Bible, King James Version, Cambridge, 1796.

Scripture quotations marked NEB are taken from New English Translation [computer file]:NET Bible.—electronic edition.—Dallas, TX: Biblical Studies Press, 1998. Used by permission. All rights reserved.

Scripture quotations marked NKJV™ are taken from the New King James Version®. Copyright © 1982 by Thomas Nelson, Inc. Used by permission. All rights reserved.

Scripture quotations marked NRSV are taken from the Holy Bible: New Revised Standard Version/Division of Christian Education of the National Council of Churches of Christ in the United States of America.—Nashville: Thomas Nelson Publishers, c 1989. Used by permission. All rights reserved.

Scripture quotations marked Phillips are taken from the New Testament in Modern English, copyright © 1958, 1959, 1960 J. B. Phillips and 1947, 1952, 1955, 1957 The Macmillian Company, New York. Used by permission. All rights reserved.

Scripture quotations marked RSV are taken from the Revised Standard Version of the Bible, copyright 1952 [2nd edition, 1971] by the Division of Christian Education of the National Council of the Churches of Christ in the United States of America. Used by permission. All rights reserved.

Printed in the United States of America

17   16   15   14   13   5   4   3   2   1

Library of Congress Control Number: 2012956244
ISBN: 978-1-62171-010-3

Cover design by Jamie Leinauer
Page design by PerfecType, Nashville, TN

SEEDBED PUBLISHING
Sowing for a Great Awakening
204 N. Lexington Avenue, Wilmore, Kentucky 40390
www.seedbed.com

TO
Ira Gallaway
Joe Hale
Eddie Fox
Danny Morris
Steve Moore
Sundo Kim
who have walked closed with me

AND TO THE MEMORY OF
Wiley Grisham
David McKeithen
Buford Dickinson
Tom Carruth
Bill Hinson
who were "giants in the land" of my spiritual journey

Contents

Preface ix
About This Study xi
Optional Introductory Group Meeting xv

Week 1: Intercession In Perspective

Day 1: The Need to Know Our Need 3
Day 2: Lord Teach Us To Pray 7
Day 3: The Essence of Intercession: Thy Kingdom Come. Thy Will Be Done. 10
Day 4: Believe that You Have Received It 14
Day 5: Developing Focus in Intercession 18
Day 6: Moses as a Model for Intercession 21
Day 7: Sacrifice Essential in Intercession 24
Group Meeting for Week One 27

Week 2: Models of Intercession in Scripture

Day 8: A Prayer Battle 29
Day 9: Persistence in Prayer 32
Day 10: The Holy Spirit and Prayer 35
Day 11: Do We Believe Our Praying Makes a Difference? 39
Day 12: Some Distortions in Thinking About Intercession 43
Day 13: Travailing: the Depth of Intercessory Prayer 46
Day 14: God Needs You 49
Group Meeting for Week Two 53

Week 3: Life in Christ

Day 15: The Indwelling Christ 57
Day 16: The Great Mystery of the Christian Faith 61
Day 17: The Secret 65
Day 18: The Vine and the Branches 68
Day 19: Greater Works Will You Do 70

Day 20: A Simple Practice With Profound Meaning 74
Day 21: The Holy Spirit Joins Us to the Risen Lord 77
Group Meeting for Week Three 80

Week 4: An Intercessory Life

Day 22: Responsible *To* or *For* Christ 83
Day 23: You are the Light of the World 86
Day 24: Recovering the Meaning of Discipleship 89
Day 25: We Are the Sent Ones 92
Day 26: Jesus' Ministry Re-presented by Christians 95
Day 27: In the Name of Christ, You Are Forgiven 97
Day 28: Intercession is Meeting on Behalf of God 101
Group Meeting for Week Four 105

Week 5: The Intercessor as Priest

Day 29: The Priesthood of All Believers 107
Day 30: Exercising Our Calling as Priests 110
Day 31: Our Identity and Purpose 113
Day 32: Over-bearing or Under-bearing 117
Day 33: The Priest as a Pattern of an Intercessory Life 121
Day 34: Responding as Priests to Two Common Needs 124
Day 35: Intercession as a Wrestling Match 128
Group Meeting for Week Five 130

Week 6: The Intercessor as Servant

Day 36: The Downward Way 133
Day 37: Compassion Party on the Road 138
Day 38: Taking Light into Dark Places 142
Day 39: The Go-Between for Reconciliation 146
Day 40: Standing in the Gap 151
Closing Group Meeting And Celebration 156

Endnotes and Works Cited 159

Preface

For many years, one of my disciplines has been what I call "keeping company with the saints." Throughout the ages there have been persons who diligently sought the Lord; many of them have shared with us through their writing. I have "kept company with them" by reading their writings. I have discovered that these individuals share some common characteristics, among which include passionate pursuit of the Lord, a thirst for holiness, and practice of disciplines—with prayer at the center of those disciplines.

The Puritan spiritual writers and preachers talked about this as "heart-work." John Flavel, a seventeenth-century English Puritan, gave this perspective: "The greatest difficulty in conversion is to win the heart to God; and the greatest difficulty after conversion is to keep the heart with God . . . heart-work is hard work indeed."[1]

The crux of heart-work is fully surrendering our will to Christ so that all we are belongs to him, and we live his life in the world.

Through the years I have written a number of workbooks, all to assist us in the heart-work essential to keep the heart with God and to grow up in Christ.

If anyone ever assesses my contribution to the church and living the Christian life, I believe they will conclude that my greatest contribution is *The Workbook of Living Prayer*. It has been translated into more than ten languages and has sold over a million copies. *Abiding in Christ: The Way of Living Prayer* is a sequel to that book. The primary dynamic of living prayer is abiding in Christ, which is the primary dynamic of the whole of the Christian life. The gracious invitation of Christ is to "abide in me." The idea of abiding in Christ offers stupendous possibility, and this workbook assists persons in making abiding in Christ the mark of *normal* Christian living.

During the past three years, I have taken the time to reflect on how my thinking and convictions about the Christian faith and way have developed. I have read through my published work over the past fifty years, along with journals and notes I have kept, and a theme has emerged: the intersection of prayer and mission, particularly one expression of prayer—intercession.

This book is an integration and summary of my thinking and of what I have written through the years. Together, we will explore intercession in the context of the whole of prayer; also as an expression of abiding in Christ. So in a sense, this book is a sequel to both *The Workbook of Living Prayer* and *Abiding in Christ: the Way of Living Prayer*.

PREFACE

Where applicable, I have included ideas, practices, and experiences I may have shared previously in these two books, as well as other writings; in this case, however the primary theme is more than prayer. Intercession is something a person *does* and *may include* or *be done through* prayer, but more than intercessory prayer, we are calling for **intercessory living.**

That's where prayer and mission intersect, and I call it **the intercessory life**. This life breaks the impossibility barrier we are constantly confronting. I believe this is the life to which all Christ followers are called and that the intercessory life is the practical, daily expression of the priesthood of all believers. I invite you to read with these convictions in mind, and pray that your involvement with and response to the teaching of his book will be the *heart-work* you need to do to make you a more dynamic participant in "the royal priesthood" of which, as a Christian, you are a part.

About This Study

OBJECTIVE: Participants grasp that intercessory living is the life to which all Christ followers are called, and that the intercessory life is a practical, daily expression of the priesthood of all believers.

INTENDED AUDIENCE: All adults

EQUIPMENT NEEDED: This book and a personal journal of your choice (purchased separately)

FORMAT: Forty-day study consisting of seven consecutive days of individual study and six group sessions (plus optional, introductory session) organized by a facilitator.

Individual study:
- Minimum ten to fifteen minutes each day
- Opens with relevant scripture passage
- Transitions to the day's lesson, supported by either anecdotal or biblical accounts
- "Reflecting and Recording"—Questions for participant to consider; these will also serve as a springboard for group sessions. This is a very important dimension of our forty-day journey. Remember when this symbol, ✢ ✢ ✢, appears, do not move on until you have responded to suggestions for reflecting and recording in your journal. Usually, this will designate a time of thoughtful quietness, meditation, reflection, and writing in your journal.
- "During the Day"—call to action that reinforces the day's lesson

Group sessions:
- Minimum sixty minutes each week (ninety minutes optimum)
- Introduction—designed to bring the group 'to order,' use our suggestions or take time to cover any housekeeping, logistics, or relevant anecdotes from the previous week
- Sharing Together—gives participants time to discuss, question, and share the thoughts and experiences they have recorded in their journals on the preceding week's lessons.
- Praying Together—gives participants the opportunity to share concerns and pray about the following week.

ABOUT THIS STUDY

FACILITATOR NOTES: To begin with, *all* participants should understand that facilitators organize, keep things moving, and serve as the point of contact for a study group; they are not 'leaders' in the sense that all knowledge, teaching, and direction comes from them. This should take pressure off of any facilitator, as their role does not come with the usual expectations that are traditionally attached to a designated 'leader.'

Group sessions are most effective when all participants talk about their experiences; as facilitator, you'll need to gauge your group's 'personality' when incorporating any of the suggestions offered here. You especially need to be sensitive to what seems to be happening in participants' lives; it is far more important for persons to be heard and feelings acknowledged than for information to be shared.

Whether you opt to open with an Introductory Session (see page xv) or wait until after the first week of individual study, you'll want to underscore a few agreed-upon specifics of confidentiality with the group during the first few sessions—if your meeting space permits, you may want to post these on the wall:

- **Keep all discussions confidential.** We gain strength and growth from sharing—this will be a safe place, built on honesty and trust. Confidentiality is expected, emphasized, and essential.
- **Treat each other with respect.** We acknowledge that our feelings are real and will not discount them in ourselves, or each other. Differences of opinion and ideas are welcome, but must be expressed in ways that do not tear down others. Respect the ideas of others.
- **Resolve conflict with maturity.** Listen attentively and wrestle with new ideas, especially those with which you disagree (the group meeting, however, should not become a debate). Should conflict arise, we will adopt the biblical approach identified in Matthew 18:15–17. Discussions will be thoughtful and move toward resolution and peace, as we are asked to do in 2 Corinthians 13:11.
- **Give everyone an opportunity.** Lift up the experiences and feelings of individuals; while the content of the study is important, applying the content to our lives and our relationship with God and others needs priority. Each one of us has a valuable voice and therefore, should have the opportunity to speak without interruption. Please give everyone an opportunity to share, if he or she desires.

- **Seek alternatives, if necessary.** If a member has sensitive needs that are beyond the scope or intent of the group, we will encourage and help this member locate an expert to meet this particular need.

If your group remains open during the entire forty-day period, you'll want to review these principles any time someone new joins the session. Group sharing is not easy; it is deceptive to pretend it is. Growth requires effort and struggle. As facilitator, don't be afraid to share your own questions, reservations, and "dry periods." As participants begin to talk honestly and openly about what is happening in their lives, group meetings will become more meaningful. This means persons will be sharing not only the good and positive, but also struggles and difficulties; therefore, everyone needs to be aware of the terms outlined above.

A Word on Corporate Prayer

Group members need to feel comfortable during corporate prayer; no one should feel pressured to pray aloud. Silent corporate prayer may be as vital and meaningful as spoken prayer. Times of silence, when thinking is centered and attention is focused, may provide our deepest periods of prayer.

Verbalizing thoughts and feelings to God in the presence of fellow pilgrims can be a powerful bonding experience for a group sharing a common journey. Verbal prayers may be offered spontaneously as persons choose to pray aloud. Avoid suggesting, "Let's go around the circle now, and each one pray." You might, however, consider having the same person open and close each prayer time. Another idea might be to ask individual group members (who are willing) to pray for the specific requests made by other individual group members, both in the shared prayer time and throughout the following week. This encourages petition and intercession at a personal level, draws groups closer together, and puts intercessory living into practice.

Additional suggestions are given each week for this "Praying Together" time; please regard these only as suggestions. What happens in the meeting—the mood, the needs expressed, the timing—should determine the direction of the group's prayer time together.

Optional Introductory Group Meeting

Therefore he is able to save completely those who come to God through him, because he always lives to intercede for them. Such a high priest meets our need—one who is holy, blameless, pure, set apart from sinners, exalted above the heavens.

—Hebrews 7:25–26

Introduction

Begin by asking each person to introduce themselves with their full name and the name by which they would like to be called. Informality is important. Encourage everyone to write the group members' names in the front of their books and pray for each one throughout the course of the study. Seek not to use titles, but use first names or nicknames as much as possible. It may be good to use nametags for the first two or three weeks. After all have introduced themselves, ask these three questions:

- Why did you become a part of the group study?
- What do you expect to gain from it?
- What are your reservations?

Let the discussion go on until about four or five have responded.

As facilitator, remind them that you are not the teacher; you serve as the contact person for the group and keep group sessions on track. Review the basic format of the individual study and group sessions and remind participants to bring their journals each week as they may need to refer to them during discussion. Reassure the group that during the "Sharing Together" component, members will be encouraged to share as they are comfortable; during "Praying Together," corporate prayer will not be forced; etc. You may also ask the group for additional input and ideas, as some members may have previous experiences in similar groups and will know what worked and what didn't; this also helps customize the sessions to fit the group's 'personality.'

And finally, as a group, confidentiality is essential; some of what may be shared could be painful or perhaps have been deeply embedded within a person for many years. Each of you owes yourselves and each other a safe environment for transparency—not only does it help the person sharing, it helps those know how to intercede on his/her behalf. You may want to spend a few minutes reviewing the confidentiality specifics on page xii. As appropriate at the weekly meetings, remind your group members of their values and commitments to each other.

Sharing Together

If time permits, take a few minutes to read the author's Preface (or, if books were obtained in advance, ask if anyone has read it already). Be willing to share with the group what is meaningful to you about his idea regarding an intercessory life; ask others to weigh in on the same. Return to the three questions asked earlier and see if, having read the Preface, any of their responses have changed or been modified.

Praying Together

Invite the group to spend a few minutes in silent prayer. Three or four minutes is a long time for people who are together for the first time, so you may want to begin with that amount of time, and increase it in the future as the group grows together. In this silence, ask the group to think of each person in the group, and what each person may have shared, and pray silently for each person.

THE INTERCESSORY LIFE

WEEK ONE
Intercession In Perspective

DAY 1

The Need to Know Our Need

*Let us hold fast the confession of our hope without wavering,
for he who promised is faithful.*

—Hebrews 10:23, RSV

IN 1991, MY WIFE AND I VISITED WHAT IS NOW THE CZECH REPUBLIC. FREEDOM from the long, painful night of Soviet oppression and persecution had only recently come. We were there to preach, teach, and offer encouragement to the faithful Christians for whom the nightmare of suffering was still a painful memory. The vivid highlight of that visit was sharing with the congregation of the Maranatha Church is Pilsen. It was one of the most exciting experiences of worship and church life in which I have ever participated.

The sanctuary of the church had been turned into a lecture hall of the university by the communist regime, but now the government had returned it to the congregation. The risers that had been built and the desks of students were still there. Over 500 people were present for worship, seventy-five percent of them younger than thirty . . . all of whom had become Christians during the past four years.

Twenty-five people had struggled as a congregation for thirty years to stay alive and the story they told was this. For over thirty years, eight women, only three of them now living, had prayed together every week. Six years previous to my visit, a young man heard about this group, joined them and the prayer group began to grow. That young man was now one of the pastors of the church, where hundreds were worshipping every week, and many young people who had grown up in a governmentally forced "atheist culture" were coming to Christian faith.

The witness of the congregation was that they were alive as a Christian congregation because of the prayers of those eight faithful women. I have never witnessed more joy, more hope, and more confidence than this people of God unashamedly dependent upon the Holy Spirit. God's presence and power was palpable. I came away rejoicing in the witness of eight women who had been faithful in intercession.

That is one of the experiences that has intensified my desire to be more faithful in intercession, an exciting dimension of our life of prayer. Let me seek to put intercession in perspective to the whole of prayer.

> No less than breathing or the sucking of a newborn infant, prayer is instinctive human behavior.

Prayer is one of the deepest impulses of the human soul. In James Baldwin's *Blues for Mister Charlie*, there is an arresting scene in which a young boy announces before his grandmother and the world that he no longer believes in God. The wise and unperturbed woman replies, "Ain't no way you can't believe in God, boy. You just try holding your breath long enough to die." No less than breathing or the sucking of a newborn infant, prayer is instinctive human behavior. Prayer is an expression of who we basically are. Certainly, as essential as eating and drinking is to our physical well-being, praying is essential to who we are as whole persons. Though quoted often, the truth of it must not be minimized by familiarity: "For thee were we made, O God, and our hearts are restless until they rest in thee." Sooner or later, sensitive to our insatiable spiritual longing and searching for fulfillment and meaning, we begin to recognize that we cannot depend upon our own resources or count on our own works to achieve meaning or grow closer to God.

Reflecting and Recording

In his first Beatitude, Jesus said those are blessed who are aware of the limitation of their own resources, and know their dependence upon God is essential to find meaning and joy. "Blessed are the poor in spirit, for theirs is the kingdom of heaven" (Matt. 5:3, NRSV).

A.W. Tozer talks about Jesus' designation of the "poor in spirit" in terms of "soul poverty," saying "the way to deeper knowledge of God is through the lonely valleys of soul poverty and abnegation of all things. The blessed ones who possess the kingdom are they who have repudiated every external thing and have rooted from their hearts all sense of possessing. These are the 'poor in spirit.' They have reached an inward state paralleling the outward circumstances of the common beggar in the streets of Jerusalem."[2]

1. On a scale of 1 to 10, 10 being completely self-sufficient, where do you find yourself?

1	2	3	4	5	6	7	8	9	10
POOR IN SPIRIT				I THINK I CAN					I KNOW I CAN

    ✤ ✤ ✤

2. Lodge the term "soul poverty" firmly in your mind. What does where you located yourself on the scale above say about "soul poverty" in your life? Spend a few minutes reflecting on this question and making some notes in your journal.

    ✤ ✤ ✤

3. One of my favorite writers, Brennan Manning, a former Catholic priest, a recovering alcoholic, and one who is painfully honest about his soul poverty, shares a challenging blessing: "May all your expectations be frustrated, may all your plans be thwarted, may all your desires be withered into nothingness, that you may experience the powerlessness and poverty of a child and sing and dance in the love of God who is Father, Son, and Spirit."[3]

Can you receive a blessing like this? What keeps you from it? Make some notes in your journal.

During the Day

As you move through the day, be sensitive and seek to be attuned to the voice of need within yourself. In those moments, rather than trying to overcome it with your own strength, try praying a prayer that expresses your dependence on God to meet that need.

DAY 2

Lord Teach Us To Pray

*He was praying in a certain place, and when he ceased,
one of his disciples said to him, "Lord, teach us to pray . . ."*

—Luke 11:1, RSV

PRAYER IS A LOT OF THINGS. IT IS PRAISE AND THANKSGIVING, CONFESSION AND contemplation. It is communion, simply being with Christ, deliberately recognizing and cultivating awareness of his presence. But at the core of it is petition and intercession. We can't think long about prayer without thinking about intercession. We can't pray very long or very often without our minds and hearts turning from our own needs and our own relationship with God to others and their needs. Whether self-consciously or intentionally, when we are at prayer we often speak the name of another, or in our thoughts we name others before God. Some of us may have never raised the question: What difference does it make? Or, does it make any difference? If it does, how does it make a difference? We continue to intercede even if we have never worked these questions through in our minds.

But there are many people who have given up prayer altogether because they do not understand or they have not seen that prayer makes a difference. Many who continue to pray have a great question mark about intercessory prayer. Even though they may be driven to name others in prayer, to call upon God to act in a certain way and bless others in special ways, they are not sure they have the right to do so. Who are they to tell God what to do? Despite the fact that they pray, they have grave reservations about the validity and effectiveness of it.

I learned a long time ago that I don't have to understand prayer, particularly intercessory prayer, to practice it. Though I have been involved in a number of well-known ministries, my name is probably more associated with *The Workbook of Living Prayer* than any thing else. The irony is I wrote the book as a novice in prayer, not as one who was an accomplished traveler on my prayer journey but as one who needed an elementary primer for my own prayer journey. I did the same thing five years later with *The Workbook of Intercessory Prayer,* expressing grave reservations about attempting such a venture, but inspired by the use that was being made of *The Workbook of Living Prayer.*

I wrote in the introduction to *The Workbook of Intercessory Prayer*:

> I am publishing this workbook on intercession with deep reservations. I'm driven by the Spirit to do it because of the need in my own life and the clamoring need of people everywhere. In doing this I risk making myself vulnerable to you who read, because I'm saying right off that in my life of intercession I have only just begun. The demands of intercessory prayer, the mystery that surrounds it, the looming questions, and my lack of total commitment and lack of proficiency—all swirl in my heart and head to intimidate and frighten me.
>
> Intercession is neither simple nor easy. So we don't walk this path without question, doubt, and reticence. I have overcome my reservation about offering this workbook, not because I have walked the path all the way, but because I want to."[4]

> We don't have to understand prayer, particularly intercessory prayer, to practice it.

Again, we don't have to understand prayer, particularly intercessory prayer, to practice it. So let's get a biblical perspective on intercessory prayer as the foundation for the call to *An Intercessory Life.*

The Lord's Prayer is the most common prayer in the Christian faith. Along with the Ten Commandments and the Apostles' Creed, Martin Luther included the Lord's Prayer as one of the three essentials for every Christian to know. Whenever Christians gather for worship, this is the prayer prayed most often. More individuals pray this prayer privately than any other. It is called the Lord's Prayer because Jesus offered it as a model when his disciples asked him to teach them to pray. It is a reliable guide for prayer.

Two essentials that we need to remember overarch the prayer. One, the God to whom we pray is good. Two, communication with God is possible. Surely God is holy and righteous and we must not ignore that. The expansive witness of Scripture is that this holy and righteous God is a God of love whose "mercy endures forever."

It is at the heart of prayer to know that God loves us, and that when we pray we are heard by Divine Love. Scripture affirms this over and over again:

- Therefore the LORD waits to be gracious to you; therefore he exalts himself to show mercy to you. (Isaiah 30:18, RSV)

- But know that the L ORD has set apart the godly for himself; the L ORD hears when I call to him. (Ps. 4:3, RSV)
- But as for me I will look to the L ORD, I will wait for the God of my salvation; my God will hear me" (Micah 7:7, RSV)
- Ask, and it will be given you; seek, and you will find; knock, and it will be opened to you. For every one who asks receives, and he who seeks finds, and to him who knocks it will be opened. (Matt. 7:7–8, RSV)

It is not likely that we are going to pray very much without the faith that God loves us and hears us. The above scriptural affirmations, climaxed by the promise of Jesus—*whoever asks receives, whoever seeks finds, and for the one who knocks the door is opened*—are clear calls to confident prayer.

Reflecting and Recording

1. In today's first paragraph we named some of the many things prayer is. Go back and read that paragraph. Write in your journal the words that describe prayer as you presently understand it.

✣ ✣ ✣

2. Now, reread the paragraph and circle the words that describe the dimensions of prayer that are most often a part of your praying. Identify why you are drawn to pray in this manner.

✣ ✣ ✣

3. How do you respond to the claim that God is good and communication with God is possible? Write a few sentences in your journal expressing your response. Do you believe it? Is there something new to you in this claim? What reservations or questions do you have about it?

During the Day

Throughout the day, remind yourself that God is good and communication with God is possible. Put this truth into practice by offering brief prayers of thanksgiving and expressions of concern for others.

DAY 3

The Essence of Intercession: Thy Kingdom Come. Thy Will Be Done.

This, then, is how you should pray: 'Our Father in heaven, hallowed be your name, your kingdom come, your will be done on earth as it is in heaven. Give us today our daily bread. And forgive us our debts, as we also have forgiven our debtors. And lead us not into temptation, but deliver us from the evil one.

—Matthew 6:9–13

THE LORD'S PRAYER IS JESUS' RESPONSE TO HIS DISCIPLES' REQUEST THAT HE teach them to pray. Jesus begins, "Our Father." This address to God supports the confidence we considered yesterday: that God is good and communication with God is possible. This was something new. As an image for God, the term "father" was present in Hebrew Scriptures, but it was a vague and sparsely used image. Yet this was Jesus' most common expression for God: *Father*. The holy and righteous God whose "mercy endures forever" is personal.

Praise and adoration are here: *Our Father in heaven, hallowed is thy name.* We have taken the "in heaven" words too literally. Jesus put an end to the idea that God is distant from us. We best think this way: It is not that where heaven is there is God, but where God is there is heaven. To pray as Jesus would have it is to pray to the God who is infinitely nearer to us even than we are to ourselves.

Our Father in heaven. Father: personal, gracious "whose mercy endures forever." In heaven: of the nearness of mind and spirit. "God is spirit: and they that worship him must worship him in spirit and in truth" (John 4:24 KJV).

Hallowed be Thy name. Before we start asking God for anything, or start telling God our sorrows and anxieties, we focus on who God is . . . God's nature, glory, love, power, holiness . . . the fact of a living presence, pervading and influencing our minds and hearts. To hallow is to praise.

DAY 3: THE ESSENCE OF INTERCESSION: THY KINGDOM COME. THY WILL BE DONE.

Also, to hallow is *to make holy*. By naming God as holy in our prayer, we place ourselves in a position to experience the majesty, mystery, and powerful presence of God.

Not only praise, and adoration, petition is here: *Give us today our daily bread*. This is asking God for the common needs of life. "The house of prayer is not a shop where we go to bargain and barter for the gifts of God. It is the home of the Father with whom we live, where all the treasures of God's love and concern are ours for the receiving."[5]

It is interesting that in the same chapter where Matthew records the Lord's Prayer, he shares the assuring words about our needs being satisfied by the Father who pays attention to the birds of the air and cares far more for us (Matt. 6:25–26).

Even so, in teaching us to offer this petition for things such as daily bread, Jesus is telling us that we need to stay aware that we are dependent upon God for all of life. So petition is here and is naturally present in our praying.

> We need to stay aware that we are dependent upon God for all of life.

Also, confession and repentance are in the prayer. *Forgive us . . . as we also have forgiven*. Implicit here is the fact that we have sinned; we have done those things that are morally wrong, breaking God's law. Some translations have it, "Forgive us our *trespasses*." To trespass means to go where we don't belong—in this case, against God, violating His will, going against persons, violating their personal rights. Whatever language we use, the very nature of forgiveness is that it has to come from beyond us, from God or from another person. Also, it has to be freely given.

The amazing truth of the gospel is that forgiveness is ours. "In Christ God was reconciling the world to himself" (2 Cor. 5:19 ESV).

The necessary movement on our part is to accept forgiveness. Accepting forgiveness leads to repentance. Overwhelmed by the love and acceptance of God, we are sorry for our sins, so forgiveness leads to repentance. It is important to note also that receiving forgiveness is dependent upon being willing to forgive. If we are having trouble receiving forgiveness it may be that we do not have a forgiving spirit. There are those we need to forgive before forgiveness can become real to us.

Note the logic of Jesus' teaching in this prayer:

We begin by focusing on God: "Our Father who are in heaven, hallowed be thy name." We continue praying for the kingdom to come on "earth as it is in heaven." The focus is still on God but is more personal in terms of God's rule in our lives and in our community. It is "God's will" for which we are asking.

Then we pray for "bread," the very sustenance of life, believing that we are dependent upon God for all of life.

Now comes the prayer for pardon: "And forgive us our debts, as we also have forgiven our debtors." Notice the word *and*, linking the prayer for pardon with the request for bread. How clear the logic! Jesus knew that God offers two kinds of food: food for the body and food for the soul; one to sustain life, the other to make life free and whole."[6]

You may have noted that in this discussion of the "movement" of the prayer, I omitted "*Thy kingdom come, thy will be done.*" I did that deliberately because our consideration of The Lord's Prayer is to make the point that intercession is at the heart of it: "Thy kingdom come, thy will be done." So we consider this petition in a more expansive way.

The prayer could not be bolder. The Kingdom of God means the reigning activity of Christ in human hearts and society. Wherever Christ's rule or reigning activity is experienced (peace, human justice, healing, shared love, reconciliation), there is the kingdom of God. To pray for the rule of Christ is a stupendous request. Yet, it is a request that our Lord taught us to make.

> To pray for the rule of Christ is a stupendous request.

The focus is beyond us. "Thy kingdom come" flows naturally from "Thy name be hallowed." That's the reason intercession is also natural and essential. We are praying for that which we desperately desire, and which we know we are impotent to accomplish within our own resources and strength. As we will discuss more fully, when we pray for a different kind of world, a world where Christ reigns, we are led into intercession for those who are not experiencing that which characterizes God's kingdom.

DAY 3: THE ESSENCE OF INTERCESSION: THY KINGDOM COME. THY WILL BE DONE.

Reflecting and Recording

1. The Kingdom of God means the reigning activity of Christ in human hearts and society. In each area, note in a few words in your journal what is missing as an expression of God's Kingdom in:

Your Own Heart (i.e., love, peace, forgiving spirit)	Society as You See It (i.e., your community, i.e. justice, compassion, reconciling spirit)

2. We pray in The Lord's Prayer "Forgive . . . as we forgive . . . " Are there persons you need to forgive before forgiveness becomes real for you? You may want to name them in your journal. Many times it helps to be that concrete in our expression.

During the Day

If possible, call or write the person or persons you named. Assure them of your forgiveness.

Continue reminding yourself that God is good and communication with God is possible, practicing that truth by offering brief prayers of thanksgiving and concern for others.

DAY 4

Believe that You Have Received It

"Have faith in God," Jesus answered. "I tell you the truth, if anyone says to this mountain, 'Go, throw yourself into the sea,' and does not doubt in his heart but believes that what he says will happen, it will be done for him. Therefore I tell you, whatever you ask for in prayer, believe that you have received it, and it will be yours. And when you stand praying, if you hold anything against anyone, forgive him, so that your Father in heaven may forgive you your sins."

—Mark 11:22–26

In his gospel, Mark recorded these few words of Jesus that summarize his teaching on prayer. Verse 24 of this passage has particular meaning for intercession: "whatever you ask for in prayer, believe that you have received it, and it will be yours."

Desire is the soul of prayer. The clarity and depth of the intensity of our desire may be the measure of how effective our intercession is. In fact, intercession is a gift for the pray-er. The possession of that gift is connected with our desire for it. Andrew Murray offers a challenging word:

> The law is unchangeable: God offers Himself, gives Himself away to the whole-hearted who give themselves wholly away to Him. He always gives us according to our heart's desire. But not as we think it, but as He sees it. If there are other desires which are more at home with us, which have our heart more than Himself and His presence, He allows these to be fulfilled and the desires that engage us at the hour of prayer cannot be granted.[7]

In prayer the desires of our heart are brought to consciousness and are expressed. Our praying is in self-awareness bringing our desires to the Lord, believing that the Lord will grant our desires. Along with desire, the second most important secret of effectual prayer is *believing*.

Only in recent years have I made the connection between the faith that is essential in knowing God, or in receiving Christ as my Savior, and the faith that is essential for a life of meaningful and powerful praying.

In our faith journey, at a given time, or in a given time frame, we simply had to *believe* and *trust* that God loved us, had given His Son for our salvation. Our assurance of salvation and our relationship to Christ were dependent upon faith.

Jesus was rather bold and expansive in underscoring faith. "'Have faith in God,' Jesus answered. 'I tell you the truth, if anyone says to this mountain, "Go, throw yourself into the sea," and does not doubt in his heart but believes that what he says will happen, it will be done for him'" (Mark 11:22–23).

As faith was essential in our entering into the Christian life, so it is with our continuing. "Believe that you have received." We don't wait for a concrete expression of God's answer; we believe we have received. It is this assurance—that God will answer—that enables us to live with the mysteries and difficulties often connected with how we perceive answers to our prayers. Again, faith must be exercised. Just as there came a time in our Christian walk when we had to simply believe and trust in God for our salvation, so we have to yield ourselves in faith and trust that God will respond to our praying. This does not mean that we will always get what we pray for. God will respond in ways that are good for us and will bring glory to him. Our stance is to pray believing—in faith.

> As faith was essential in our entering into the Christian life, so it is with our continuing.

Too many have lost touch with those early experiences in our spiritual journeys when we took steps of faith on our way to salvation. Remembering and rehearsing these experiences enriches our faith and gives us courage to take new steps of faith.

One other word of perspective. Intercession is a ministry of the whole church as the Body of Christ. The prayer ministry of the church is in fact the very prayer life of our Lord. The writer of Hebrews describes Jesus as the one "who lives to make intercession." Our Lord intercedes for us in glory, and that works itself out by the Spirit of God interceding through the groaning intercessions of the people of God.

Jack Hayford expressed it succinctly: "Prayer is essentially a partnership of the redeemed child of God working hand in hand with God toward the realization of His redemptive purposes on earth."[8]

This partnership guarantees God's presence, which is the source of all power in praying.

God's presence to us is a great central promise of Scripture. What the psalmist experienced—". . . I walk through the valley of the shadow of death, I will fear no evil, for you are with me,"(Ps. 23:4)—was given everlasting meaning as Jesus concluded his Great Commission: "Surely I am with you always, to the very end of he age" (Matt. 28:20). Powerful intercession comes through the person who lives consciously "hidden with Christ in God." This is the fundamental requirement of an intercessory life on which we will focus in weeks 4, 5, and 6—to abide in Christ by recognizing, cultivating awareness of, and giving expression to the indwelling Christ.

Again, unfathomable mystery is here, but mystery we can claim boldly as Christians. We have been given the privilege of being connected intimately to God, primarily through our abiding in Christ. There is unspeakable joy in this privilege, but there is also the power to be used by God as instruments of making all persons his dwelling place, and all creation showing his glory. Intercession is one of the chief channels and means of grace through which the Father does his work in the world. The awesome fact is that intercession, unceasing intercession, opens the doors of heaven for the Father's blessings to flow and for persons to become partakers of those blessings. The intercession of God's people is a huge instrument in the coming of God's Kingdom and the doing of God's will on earth as it is in heaven. (Matt. 6:10)[9]

Reflecting and Recording

1. What are three or three or four of your deepest desires? Record them in your journal.

✣ ✣ ✣

2. Spend some time examining these desires in light of the fact that ***desire is the soul of prayer.*** Is any of these desires greater than your desire to be in the presence of God and God's will? If these desires were granted would you be closer to or further from God?

✣ ✣ ✣

3. Recall in your faith journey when you simply believed and trusted God for your salvation. What was going on in your life? What led you to your faith commitment?

DAY 4: BELIEVE THAT YOU HAVE RECEIVED IT

✣ ✣ ✣

4. Looking back at your reflection on believing in and trusting Christ for salvation, are you believing and trusting in that fashion in your praying? Spend some time examining your prayer life in this light. Are you moved or convicted to change this? Why or why not?

―――――――――――― During the Day ――――――――――――

Memorizing Scripture is a discipline we need to recover. As Christians, we are to live by the word. We can't be people of prayer without being people of the word. Memorizing Scripture enables us to "hide" some of God's word in our hearts; that word becomes a source of unexpected guidance, strength, and inspiration in times of need. Throughout these forty days, I will suggest verses of Scripture for you to commit to memory. The first comes from the *Epistle to the Hebrews*. This book is a great description of Jesus Christ as God Incarnate, one of us, Priest, Sacrifice, and Coming Messiah. In chapters 4–8, particularly, the writer magnificently portrays Jesus as our great "High Priest." In chapter 7, he explains that many other priests who came before Jesus were prevented from continuing as priests because they died. But Jesus was distinct, because he was Divine and conquered death so Christ as Priest continues forever. His priesthood is unchangeable, therefore "He is able to save to the uttermost those who come to God through Him, since He ever lives to make intercession for them" (7:25 NKJV).

You may want to copy this verse on a card so you can carry it with you throughout the days ahead to read it at every opportunity or your memorization process.

DAY 5

Developing Focus in Intercession

We know that the whole creation has been groaning as in the pains of childbirth right up to the present time. Not only so, but we ourselves, who have the firstfruits of the Spirit, groan inwardly as we wait eagerly for our adoption to sonship, the redemption of our bodies. For in this hope we were saved. But hope that is seen is no hope at all. Who hopes for what they already have? But if we hope for what we do not yet have, we wait for it patiently. In the same way, the Spirit helps us in our weakness. We do not know what we ought to pray for, but the Spirit himself intercedes for us through wordless groans. And he who searches our hearts knows the mind of the Spirit, because the Spirit intercedes for God's people in accordance with the will of God.

—Romans 8:22–27

THE DEFEAT AND DISSOLUTION OF APARTHEID IN SOUTH AFRICA WAS ONE OF the most remarkable national developments of any country in the twentieth century. Though it is still suffering the terrible fall-out of the horrendous system of apartheid, when I visited the country, I found the church alive and well in the context of challenging circumstances that would normally evoke despair. I was inspired by the commitment, the perseverance, the joyful worship, and the compassion that is unabated by what seems an impossible, unchangeable situation.

At every worship gathering I was in, they lit a candle on the altar and prayed this prayer: "God bless Africa, guard her children, guide her leaders, and grant her peace."

Throughout the terrible and painful years of apartheid, the Methodist Church played an influential role in opposition to the oppressive apartheid system. They organized and acted; they demonstrated and worked; and they prayed. My friend Peter Storey was the bishop and longtime pastor of the Central Mission in downtown Johannesburg. On the altar in the sanctuary of that church, there was a large candle, surrounded by a coil of barbed wire. It was beautiful and ghastly at the same time—a lovely candle with snarling wire biting out of it.

DAY 5: DEVELOPING FOCUS IN INTERCESSION

Every Sunday, the people would pray for South Africa and the dismantling of apartheid. They read the names of those who were in prison in opposition to the system and committed themselves afresh to justice. Then they would light the candle. Suddenly, amidst those cruel coils of barbed wire the light would come alive, and those Christians would remember the words of scripture: "The light shines in the darkness, and the darkness has never put it out."

That congregation knew and claimed her identity as "a city set upon a hill which could not be hid" (Matt. 5:14). I remembered the practice of that Johannesburg congregation and the long years of persevering prayer when I joined with worshipers, continuing to pray, "God bless Africa, guard her children, guide her leaders, and give her peace."

It is the witness of the church in South Africa, the church in Eastern Europe and the former Soviet Union, the church in China and Cuba that prayer has been the sustaining power, giving courage, and yes, transforming circumstances.

> As we move more deeply into intercession, we can imagine ourselves as a part of a great procession approaching the throne of grace. We are not alone.

To intercede is to worship God. When we worship, we move into the presence of God . . . praising, offering thanks and adoration, listening in humility, confessing and repenting. Christ is the center of our worship. Christ on the cross is history's great act of intercession, transforming circumstances for all humankind, for all *space-time continuum.*

You see, intercession is personal and often private, but private not in the sense of individualistic, one-person activity. As we move more deeply into intercession, we can imagine ourselves as a part of a great procession approaching the throne of grace. We are not alone. As we lay our burdens on the altar, we are preparing ourselves for, and hopefully committing ourselves to an intercessory life.

Intercession, then, is at the heart of our relationship to the Father, the risen and reigning Christ, and the Holy Spirit. Two verses combine to give the picture.

Romans 8:27 says, God, "who searches hearts knows what is the mind of the Spirit, because the Spirit intercedes for the saints according to the will of God." Put that with the exhilarating fact that Christ "always lives to make intercession" for us (Heb. 7:25), and you have the dynamic work of the Trinity . . . Father, Son, and Holy Spirit. God searches our minds and the Holy Spirit becomes the intercessor of our hearts. Our intercessions, through the Holy Spirit, become one with Christ, who is the Great Intercessor in the throne room of heaven.

Reflecting and Recording

1. Re-read today's opening scripture (Rom. 8:22–27) two or three times and reflect on it by paying attention to the language as it relates to prayer. Does "adoption to sonship" say anything about our relationship to God, and the fact that God is good, and that communication with God is possible?

⬥ ⬥ ⬥

2. Does "wordless groans" suggest anything essential to our praying?

⬥ ⬥ ⬥

3. How have you experienced the Spirit helping you "in weakness"?

⬥ ⬥ ⬥

4. What does it mean by "the Spirit himself intercedes for us"?

⬥ ⬥ ⬥

5. Is there something 'too big' for your prayers that you wish you could change on a local, regional, national, or global scale?

During the Day

Continue memorizing and living with the scripture suggested yesterday.

DAY 6

Moses as a Model for Intercession

*Moses was faithful as a servant in all God's house,
testifying to what would be said in the future.*

—Hebrews 3:5

One of the most familiar persons in the Old Testament is Moses. He was both a priest and a prophet to Israel. A priest speaks to God for the people and to the people for God. Moses did that. His notable work was that he confronted Pharaoh and led his people out of Egyptian bondage.

One of the most dramatic events in that Exodus journey was the miraculous crossing of the Red Sea. Following that watershed experience, every day was marked by signs of God's guidance and care. There was manna for food that came "fresh every morning." Crystal waters had gushed from rocks. A fleecy cloud shaded them from the blistering sun and guided them during the day, and when darkness came there was a subdued but radiant cloud of light shining over their camp.

Over and over again, God displayed his providential care and Israel pledged their loyalty to God and to keeping the law. But now, barely three months since the crossing on dry land over the Red Sea, they were at the foot of Sinai, the luminous cloud/Presence still brooding over them, and Moses goes up the mountain to meet with God. "When the people saw that Moses was so long in coming down from the mountain, they gathered around Aaron and said, 'Come, make us gods who will go before us. As for this fellow Moses who brought us up out of Egypt, we don't know what has happened to him'" (Ex. 32:1). Aaron commands them to bring their jewelry and he used the gold to cast an image of a calf. The people claimed this idol as their god, and Aaron built an altar and called for a festival.

Meanwhile, up on Mount Sinai, God told Moses about this sinful action and commanded him to go down at once and confront this "stiff-necked" people who were acting so perversely. After outlining how Moses was to confront the people, God said to Moses, "Now leave me alone so that my anger may burn against them and that I may destroy them. Then I will make you into a great nation" (Ex. 32:10).

Moses cannot bear the thought. Even with the promise that he, Moses, would be protected and in some other way "made into a great nation," he is not willing to accept God's verdict without an argument, without interceding on behalf of this "stiff-necked people" for whom he had already risked everything to lead.

> But Moses sought the favor of the LORD his God. "LORD," he said, "why should your anger burn against your people, whom you brought out of Egypt with great power and a mighty hand? Why should the Egyptians say, 'It was with evil intent that he brought them out, to kill them in the mountains and to wipe them off the face of the earth'? Turn from your fierce anger; relent and do not bring disaster on your people. Remember your servants Abraham, Isaac and Israel, to whom you swore by your own self: 'I will make your descendants as numerous as the stars in the sky and I will give your descendants all this land I promised them, and it will be their inheritance forever.'" Then the LORD relented and did not bring on his people the disaster he had threatened.—Exodus 32:11–14

How we perceive God's nature determines how we pray. Moses was bold in his intercession because he knew God's nature and character. So, he intercedes, reminding God of God's covenant, and in verse 14, we have this surprising word in the story: "Then the Lord repented and did not bring on his people the disaster he had threatened."

> How we perceive God's nature determines how we pray.

Some who think they have to be rigidly consistent in a description of God as sovereign, transcendent, and immovable might want to downplay this verse as an unimportant detail in the story, a vestige of an outgrown phase of religion. But not so; this is revelation, and is at the very heart of the story.

The grand narrative of Scripture is of a God of mercy, one who hears the prayers of God's people and responds in compassion. One of the ways you can read the history of Israel in the Old Testament is that of God getting angry at Israel, threatening to punish, to abandon, even to destroy her, but—remembering the covenant made with Abraham, Isaac, and Jacob—He relents, forgives, and takes Israel back.

DAY 6: MOSES AS A MODEL FOR INTERCESSION

We must remember this when we pray. Moses appeals to the nature of God to keep faith with God's promise and covenant. He knew the history and character of God, indeed he had been an active part of that history. He also knew better than anyone else the perversity and sin of his own people, but he refused to allow his relationship with those "stiff-necked people" to end. Because of his intercession, different translations of Scripture have it, "the Lord *repented, relented or changed his mind* about the disaster he had planned to bring on his people" (Ex. 32:14).

Reflecting and Recording

1. How does the fact that Scriptue says the Lord "repented," "relented," or "changed his mind" harmonize with your understanding of God's nature? Is this a new thought for you? Which one of the translations do you prefer: repented, relented, or changed his mind? Why?

✤ ✤ ✤

2. Spend a few minutes reflecting on the nature and charcter of God in light of Moses' experience with God.

✤ ✤ ✤

During the Day

Continue living with the memory verse. Have you memorized it yet?

DAY 7

Sacrifice Essential in Intercession

The next day Moses said to the people, "You have committed a great sin. But now I will go up to the LORD; perhaps I can make atonement for your sin."

—Exodus 32:30

LATER IN YESTERDAY'S STORY FROM EXODUS 32, GOD MAKES IT CLEAR WHO GOD is. Moses is in the high mountains with splintered peaks around, in one of his regular one on one conversations with God, and asks God to "show him his glory." The Lord instructs him to move into the cleft in the rock and says, "I will cause my goodness to pass in front of you, and I will proclaim my name, the Lord, in your presence. I will have mercy on whom I will have mercy, and will have compassion on whom I will have compassion" (Ex. 33:19). F. B. Meyer, British scholar/preacher, makes this observation:

> There was nothing in the brooding cloud, or flashing light, or trembling earth to stimulate the sense of loving kindness and tender mercy (in God). Yet Moses seems to have come to the very discovery of God as John did, after being trained in the inner secret of Christ's love, and they reached hands across the centuries—Moses the shepherd of Israel and John the disciple whom Jesus loved—saying 'God is Love.'[10]

When God revealed his goodness and mercy to Moses, this intensified Moses praying; he stayed on the mountain, pleading for his people for forty days and nights. Persistence, what is called *importunity* in the New Testament, which we will discuss later, is an essential dimension of intercession.

Return to Moses' intercession for Israel following the golden calf sin of idolatry, putting another god before God:

> Moses saw that the people were running wild and that Aaron had let them get out of control and so became a laughingstock to their enemies . . . The next day Moses said to the people 'You have

committed a great sin. But now I will go up the Lord; perhaps I can make atonement for your sin . . . So Moses went back to the Lord and said 'Oh, what a great sin these people have committed! They have made themselves gods of gold. But now, please forgive their sin—but if not, then blot me out of the book you have written." (Ex. 32: 25, 30–33)

Genuine intercession is unselfish, even sacrificial. Moses had interceded with God earlier and had convinced God not to destroy the people. Now he announces to them that he will mediate for them again. And what a dramatic encounter it was! There is not much detail about what must have gone on between Moses and God, but there was no need for that. The jolting fact, found in verse 33, was that Moses was willing to give his own life for his people: "If you won't forgive their sins, then blot me out."

> Genuine intercession is unselfish, even sacrificial.

This sacrificial intercessory commitment reminds us of Jesus and his praying. Though the prayers of Jesus verbally reported in the gospels are not many, his unselfish intercession is convincing. When we discuss it later, we will label it *willing love,* which is an essential dimension for effective intercession. One thinks of what we call Jesus' "high priestly prayer" in John 17, and his commitment, "for their sakes I sanctify Myself" (v. 19 NKJV). This unselfish intercession reached the ultimate height in Jesus' willingness to go to the cross on our behalf, and even there, interceding for his enemies: "Father, forgive them; for they know not what they do" (Luke 23:34 KJV).

Was what he would do with his Son in God's mind as he listened to Moses' pleading and witnessed the earnestness of his prayers in his willingness to die for his people? In essence, God's response was that every man must stand for his own sin. Moses could not make an atonement for he, too, was a sinner, and no sinful person can make an atonement for another. Yet, in mercy and in the love that would one day give Christ to the cross, forgiveness was granted. Moses affirmed his call to lead the people to the land of promise, with God's assurance that God's angel would go before them. Moses knew his prayer had been answered. We may not always "know" as clearly as Moses, but trusting God we will know that he is with us.

Reflecting and Recording

1. The thesis of this book is that intercession is a form of prayer to which we are called, but prayer in only one expression of intercession. The ultimate call is to an intercessory life. Look back over your life and recall an experience in which you prayed, acted, or related sacrificially to another. Make enough notes in your journal of your memory of that experience to get it clearly in mind.

2. Would you think of that experience as intercession? What about it suggests the nature of intercessory prayer?

During the Day

Jesus affirmed in prayer, "for their sakes I sanctify myself." This was the height of unselfish commitment. Keep this word in mind as you share with people today and in the coming days. If you are a part of a group sharing this workbook journey, keep this word in mind as you participate in meeting with them today.

Group Meeting for Week One

Introduction

Group sessions are most effective when all participants talk about their experiences; this guide is designed to facilitate personal sharing. All participants need to be sensitive to what seems to be happening in each other's lives; it is far more important for persons to be heard and feelings acknowledged than for information to be shared. If you did not opt for the Introductory Session, you may want to review and pull in some of the elements for this session.

And finally, as a group, be mindful that confidentiality is essential. Each of you owes yourselves and each other a safe environment for transparency—not only does it help the person sharing, it helps those know how to intercede on his/her behalf.

Sharing Together

If you did not have an introductory session to get acquainted, begin by asking each person to introduce themselves, giving their full name and the name by which they would like to be called. Informality is important. If you did opt for the introductory session, be sure to introduce any new members who have arrived this week.

- As a group, spend four or five minutes responding to this question: What is your response to the author's (Maxie's) claim that God is good and communication with God is possible?
- Invite the group to thumb through the workbook and locate their most difficult or most meaningful day with the material. Then ask three or four volunteers to share either their most meaningful, or most difficult day. You, the facilitator, will want to begin the sharing.
- Invite the group to turn to their Reflecting and Recording on Day 6 of their book. Spend as much time as you have left discussing the nature of God in light of Moses experience of God "repenting" (relenting or changing his mind). Is this a new insight? What do you think about it?

Praying Together

Each week's suggestions call for the group to pray together. Corporate prayer empowers Christians. This is a huge part of our 40-day Journey.

As a reminder, group members need to feel comfortable during corporate prayer. No one should feel pressured to pray aloud. Silent corporate prayer may be as vital and meaningful as spoken prayer.

That said, verbalizing thoughts and feelings to God in the presence of fellow pilgrims can be a powerful bonding experience for a group sharing a common journey. Verbal prayers may be offered spontaneously as persons choose to pray aloud. Avoid suggesting, "Let's go around the circle now, and each one pray." You might, however, consider having the same person open and close each prayer time. Another idea might be to ask individual group members (who are willing) to pray for the specific requests made by other individual group members, both in the shared prayer time and throughout the following week. This encourages petition and intercession at a personal level, draws groups closer together, and puts intercessory living into practice.

Here are some possibilities for this closing period:

- If you have not already done so, encourage everyone to write the names of group members in the front of their book and to pray for them every week.
- Invite the group to spend a few minutes in silent prayer. Three or four minutes is a long time for people who are together for the first time, so you may want to begin with that amount of time, and increase it in the future as the group grows together. In this silence, ask the group to think of each person in the group, and what each person may have shared, and pray silently for each person.
- Ask a volunteer to close by praying aloud the Brennan Manning prayer at the close of Day One.

WEEK TWO
Models of Intercession in Scripture

DAY 8

A Prayer Battle

Answer me, O LORD, answer me, so these people will know that you, O LORD, are God, and that you are turning their hearts back again.

—1 Kings 18:37

INTERCESSION IS A PROMINENT PART OF THE OLD TESTAMENT STORY. THERE were many intercessors in Israel, none more prominent than Moses, but the prophet Elijah plays a major role and teaches us an important lesson about how God uses persons to accomplish his will through prayer.

One of the most dramatic accounts in scripture can be found in the eighteenth chapter of 1 Kings. The prophet Elijah is the central human character; God, however, is the main character because this is a showdown that identifies who really is the one true God.

The prophet Elijah models an intercessory life; he speaks to the people for God and to God for the people. More often than not, we don't want to hear the prophet's words . . . words of truth that are often words of judgment and condemnation, as confirmed by King Ahab, who greets Elijah with, "Is that you, you troubler of Israel?" (v.17)

For more than two years, no rain had fallen, and the country was in a severe drought. In essence, Elijah pointed his finger at King Ahab and said, "Your idolatry and the wickedness of you and Queen Jezebel . . . you are the cause of the drought." To prove his point, Elijah challenged the prophets of Baal, all 450 prophets of them, to a test on Mount Carmel:

> Then Elijah said to them, "I am the only one of the LORD's prophets left, but Baal has four hundred and fifty prophets. Get two bulls for us. Let them choose one for themselves, and let them cut it into pieces and put it on the wood but not set fire to it. I will prepare the other bull and put it on the wood but not set fire to it. Then you call on the name of your god, and I will call on the name of the LORD. The god who answers by fire—he is God." Then all the people said, "What you say is good."—1 Kings 18:22–24

The prophets of Baal went first. They prayed from morning until afternoon, but to no avail. Try as they might, they could not get Baal to send the fire they needed. Late in the afternoon, it was finally Elijah's turn. He repaired the altar that was broken down, taking twelve stones representing the twelve tribes of Israel and built them into an altar to God. Then a trench was dug around it. Wood for the fire was laid. A young bull which had been cut into pieces was put upon the altar. Twelve barrels of water, the equivalent of ninety-six gallons, were poured upon the altar and its sacrifice. That amount of water would say to the king that God had something to say about drought. But also that amount of water on the wood and the sacrifice would say something to those who looked on: "How can there be fire with that kind of water saturating everything?"

> Sometimes, the spectacular blinds us to the significant, underpinning truth.

Elijah prayed and fire fell from heaven. What a spectacle! It had to be a great fire, because it evaporated all the water in the trench around the altar and consumed the water-logged sacrifice.

There are all sorts of lessons here but sometimes, the spectacular blinds us to the significant, underpinning truth. In this instance, it is the truth that God uses persons to accomplish his will through prayer as well as action. In the first verse of the story, after three years of drought (which was God's judgment), God spoke to Elijah, "Go, show yourself to Ahab, and I'll send rain on the face of the earth." Then at the end of the story, after several other events have occurred, Elijah prays seven times and finally, the rain comes.

Did you miss it? Whose idea was it to send rain? Who took the initiative? Whose will was it? It was God's—not Elijah's. We will discuss this more fully, but register the truth clearly: God chooses to do *His* work and accomplish *His* will through people. *There are some things God either cannot or will not do until and unless people pray.*

If ending the drought was God's idea, will, and timing, why did it take Elijah's intervention and praying to bring the rain? Why did Elijah have to pray seven times? God chose that way. It is a part of God's sovereign plan . . . to use persons to accomplish His will. Sometimes, it is the work (action) of persons that will accomplish His will; but sometimes, it is the prayers of His people.

That's the significant underlining truth behind the spectacular story of Elijah's battle with the gods of Baal: God chooses to use us and our praying to accomplish His will.

Reflecting and Recording

1. What are the first thoughts that come to your mind in response to the statement, *There are some things God either cannot or will not do until and unless people pray.* Make some notes in your journal.
2. Looking back over your life, can you remember an occasion when you prayed about a situation or for a person and change came? If so, can you affirm that God was using you and your praying to accomplish his will?

✣ ✣ ✣

During the Day

As you move through the day let this affirmation register in your mind as a challenge and call to prayer: *There are some things God either cannot or will not do until and unless people pray.*

DAY 9

Persistence in Prayer

And he told them a parable, to the effect that they ought always to pray and not lose heart.

—Luke 18:1, RSV

In my growing up years in rural Mississippi, one of the gospel songs we would sing was entitled *Showers of Blessing*:

Showers of blessing
Showers of blessing we need
Mercy drops round us are falling
But for the showers we plead.

Sometimes in our praying we too quickly settle for "mercy drops" when God wants to give "showers."

Yesterday, we focused our attention on Elijah. The significant, underlining truth behind the spectacular story of his battle with the prophets of Baal is that God chooses to use us and our praying to accomplish His will. Seven times Elijah prayed; seven is the biblical number of completion. God was teaching us that we must pray until the work is done.

Our consideration of Elijah and his persistence is a good segue to the witness of prayer in the life of the New Testament church and the power of prayer in individuals and the Christian community. In Luke 18, Jesus tells one of his parables to teach his disciples that they "should always pray and not give up" (v. 1). In sum, a widow kept coming to a judge who "neither feared God nor cared for men," pleading for justice against an adversary. The widow kept coming and pleading, but the judge kept refusing to hear her and respond.

Finally, the judge confesses that he can no longer bear the woman's pleading, and says, "I will see that she gets justice, so that she won't eventually wear me out by her coming" (v. 5). Jesus then offers the lesson of the parable: "Listen to what the unjust judge says: 'And will not God bring about justice for his chosen ones, who cry out to him day and night? Will he keep putting them off? I tell you, he will see that they get justice, and quickly" (v. 6–8).

Persistence is necessary, but let's not make the mistake of thinking that persistence is to overcome the reluctance of God. We must not identify God with the calloused judge in the parable. God wills to do what is right and good, and we are to have faith that God will do what we are asking. Paul calls us to "be faithful in prayer"(Rom. 12:12) and to "always keep on praying" (Eph. 6:18).

> Sometimes in our praying we too quickly settle for "mercy drops" when God wants to give "showers."

Look now at The Acts of the Apostles for a powerful witness. Acts is the story of the birth and life of the church in the years immediately after Jesus' death, resurrection, and ascension. My friend, Lloyd Ogilvie, outstanding preacher, writer, and one-time chaplain of the U.S. Senate, described the first chapter of Acts as the account of what happened between the "lightning of the incarnation of Christ and the thunder of Pentecost." He got the image from his fascination as a boy with the amount of time that elapsed between the lightning and thunder that punctuated thunderstorms. He and his young friends would count the seconds between the brilliant flashes of light and the turbulent rumble of thunder caused by the heating and expansion of the air along the line of the lightning flash. They would argue about which they liked best. Lloyd said he supported a case for thunder without lightning. One day his father overheard the discussion and said, "Son, you can't have the thunder without the lightning."

Thus Lloyd's image of the lightning of the incarnation and the thunder of Pentecost: "The two cannot be separated. The birth, life, ministry, teaching, death, resurrection, ascension, and the return of the Lord in the infilling, infusing power of the Holy Spirit are all part of the cosmic atonement and the birth of the new Israel, the church."[11]

The risen Lord had promised, "You will receive power when the Holy Spirit comes on you," (Acts 1:8). The promise became reality as a result of prayer: "When the day of Pentecost came, they were all together in one place. Suddenly a sound like the blowing of a violent wind came from heaven and filled the whole house where they were sitting. They saw what seemed to be tongues of fire that separated and came to rest on each of them. All of them were filled with the Holy Spirit." (Acts 2:1–5)

When Jesus was trying to prepare his disciples for his death, he told them that he would see them again, their grief would be taken away and they would rejoice. He then added, "In that day you will no longer ask me anything. I tell you the truth, my Father will give you whatever you ask in my name" (John 16:23).

"That day" had come, and Holy Spirit power was poured out upon them.

Contemplating this experience, one remembers another promise of Jesus: "Which of you fathers, if your son asks for a fish, will give him a snake instead? Or if he asks for an egg, will give him a scorpion? If you then, though you are evil, know how to give good gifts to your children, how much more will your Father in heaven give the Holy Spirit to those who ask him!" (Luke 11:11–13).

The "thunder of Pentecost" had come because "these all continued with one accord in prayer and supplication" (Acts. 1:14 KJV). That continuing in prayer provides the dynamic of Acts.

Reflecting and Recording

The witness of Scripture is clear: One, Jesus and early Christian leaders taught that persistence in prayer is essential; two, the Holy Spirit gave birth to the church. Spend some time reflecting on the community of faith of which you are a part.

- Is there much teaching about the Holy Spirit?
- How do you see the Holy Spirit at work?
- What role does the Holy Spirit play in your worship?

During the Day

Continue to be inspired and challenged by the claim, *There are some things God either cannot or will not do until and unless people pray.*

DAY 10

The Holy Spirit and Prayer

And the believers from among the circumcised who came with Peter were amazed, because the gift of the Holy Spirit had been poured out even on the Gentiles.

—Acts 10:45, RSV

Today, we'll look at some of the specific instances of that thundering power of the Holy Spirit that comes through prayer about which we began to share yesterday.

The organization of the early church was simply the result of the disciples praying and following the flow of the Holy Spirit. Here is a concrete illustration of it:

> In those days when the number of disciples was increasing, the Hellenistic Jews among them complained against the Hebraic Jews because their widows were being overlooked in the daily distribution of food. So the Twelve gathered all the disciples together and said, "It would not be right for us to neglect the ministry of the word of God in order to wait on tables. Brothers and sisters, choose seven men from among you who are known to be full of the Spirit and wisdom. We will turn this responsibility over to them and will give our attention to prayer and the ministry of the word.
>
> This proposal pleased the whole group. They chose Stephen, a man full of faith and of the Holy Spirit; also Philip, Procorus, Nicanor, Timon, Parmenas, and Nicolas from Antioch, a convert to Judaism. They presented these men to the apostles, who prayed and laid their hands on them.
>
> So the word of God spread. The number of disciples in Jerusalem increased rapidly, and a large number of priests became obedient to the faith—Acts 6:1–7

Dissention had risen in the community because some folks were being neglected in the distribution of alms. The disciples proposed that deacons would be appointed to do that serving work, and "We," they said, "will give ourselves continually to prayer, and to the ministry of the word." They saw clearly that their ministry of the word, their leadership of the community required prayer.

They had to order the life of the community in such a way as to give them the time for that essential work of prayer.

> The praying of these two men—their visions that came through prayer—radically changed the shape and direction of the Christian movement.

Another witness to the place of prayer in the life of the disciples and the early church is the account of the turning point in Peter's ministry. It happened in relation to Cornelius, who with all his family "were devout and God-fearing."

One day at about three in the afternoon he had a vision. He distinctly saw an angel of God, who came to him and said, "Cornelius!" Cornelius stared at him in fear. "What is it, Lord?" he asked. The angel answered, "Your prayers and gifts to the poor have come up as a memorial offering before God. Now send men to Joppa to bring back a man named Simon who is called Peter. He is staying with Simon the tanner, whose house is by the sea." When the angel who spoke to him had gone, Cornelius called two of his servants and a devout soldier who was one of his attendants. He told them everything that had happened and sent them to Joppa."—Acts 10:3–8

Note the merging of prayer in the life of two persons. On the next day, when Cornelius' servants were on their way to find him:

Peter went up on the roof to pray. He became hungry and wanted something to eat, and while the meal was being prepared, he fell into a trance. He saw heaven opened and something like a large sheet being let down to earth by its four corners. It contained all kinds of four-footed animals, as well as reptiles and birds. Then a voice told him, "Get up, Peter. Kill and eat." "Surely not, Lord!" Peter replied. "I have never eaten anything impure or unclean." The voice spoke to him a second time, "Do not call anything impure that God has made clean."

This happened three times, and immediately the sheet was taken back to heaven."—Acts 10:9–16

Cornelius' men found Peter still wondering about the meaning of his vision. They told him about Cornelius' vision and his invitation for Peter to come and share God's message with him and his people. The praying of these two men—their visions that came through prayer—radically changed the shape and direction of the Christian movement.

DAY 10: THE HOLY SPIRIT AND PRAYER

Peter began to share the gospel message with Cornelius and his people, and:

While Peter was still speaking these words, the Holy Spirit came on all who heard the message. The circumcised believers who had come with Peter were astonished that the gift of the Holy Spirit had been poured out even on the Gentiles. For they heard them speaking in tongues and praising God. Then Peter said, "Can anyone keep these people from being baptized with water? They have received the Holy Spirit just as we have." So he ordered that they be baptized in the name of Jesus Christ—Acts 10:44–48

This was the decisive turning point in the life of the church. The prayers of two men bring a blessing beyond all expectation. The gospel message would now be taken to all persons; the grace of God was for Gentiles as well as Jews.

Reflecting and Recording

Yesterday, you were asked to reflect on the role the Holy Spirit plays in the life of the community of faith of which you are a part. Continue that reflection.

- What role does the Holy Spirit play in your decision-making about program and mission?
- Leadership?
- The ordering of your ongoing life together?

For now, and for future reference, it will be meaningful to make some notes in your journal.

❖ ❖ ❖

Recall an occasion/situation when your community of faith, as a body, prayed for guidance and direction. Again, making notes in your journal will be meaningful.

❖ ❖ ❖

The turning point in the life of the early Church was when the conviction came that God's grace was for Gentiles as well as Jews; the gospel message would now be taken to all persons. Spend your closing time thinking about the people in your community to which the Church may be paying little or no attention. Pray about how your community of faith may respond.

❖ ❖ ❖

During the Day

As you move throughout the day, continue thinking about who in your community are those with whom the gospel needs most to be shared.

DAY 11

Do We Believe Our Praying Makes a Difference?

So Peter was kept in prison, but the church was earnestly praying to God for him. The night before Herod was to bring him to trial, Peter was sleeping between two soldiers, bound with two chains, and sentries stood guard at the entrance. Suddenly an angel of the Lord appeared and a light shone in the cell. He struck Peter on the side and woke him up. "Quick, get up!" he said, and the chains fell off Peter's wrists. Then the angel said to him, "Put on your clothes and sandals." And Peter did so. "Wrap your cloak around you and follow me," the angel told him. Peter followed him out of the prison, but he had no idea that what the angel was doing was really happening; he thought he was seeing a vision. They passed the first and second guards and came to the iron gate leading to the city. It opened for them by itself, and they went through it. When they had walked the length of one street, suddenly the angel left him. Then Peter came to himself and said, "Now I know without a doubt that the Lord has sent his angel and rescued me from Herod's clutches and from everything the Jewish people were hoping would happen."

—Acts 12:5–11

It should be obvious that prayer was prominent in the early church and prayer is connected with the Holy Spirit and power. No prayer, no Holy Spirit; no Holy Spirit—no prayer and no power.

The above Scripture is a part of a dramatic story. As always, the context is important. King Herod, the grandson of the Herod who presided over the slaughter of the innocent children when Jesus was born, is now persecuting the church. This Herod not only inherited his grandfather's name, but also seems to have inherited his violent nature, The Bible says that he "laid violent hands upon some who belonged to the church." One of those was James. Herod arrested James and ordered his execution. When there was no great public outcry against this execution, he decided to do the same with Peter, the leader of the Christian community in Jerusalem.

Peter was scheduled for the same sort of execution that James experienced. However, on the very night that he was to meet his death, he was sleeping, bound in chains, guards inside and outside his cell. An angel appeared in the cell, called for Peter to get up, and when Peter did, mysteriously his chains fell off. The angel instructed him to put on his cloak and sandals and follow him.

> Many times we pray, not expecting anything to happen.

Peter thought he was dreaming; this couldn't be actually happening. He soon became convinced, however, when the cell door was opened, and he followed the angel down a corridor. At the end of the corridor, there was an iron gate that was kept locked at all times. But when Peter and the angel reached the second guard post, the Iron Gate it swung open. As the Bible puts it, "it opened for them of its own accord" (v. 10).

When Peter was finally out on the street, he realized what was happening. He said to himself, "Now I know it is true. The Lord has sent his angel and rescued me from Herod's clutches" (v. 11).

Peter knew immediately where he was to go. His friends had gathered in the house of one of the believers and were holding an all night prayer vigil for him. They knew how desperate the situation was and there didn't seem to be much they could do about it. They were no match for Herod and the authorities. The one thing they could do, though, was pray. No one left the prayer meeting early that night; they kept on praying during those long, sad hours.

The story gets a bit humorous at this point. When Peter knocked at the door, a young woman named Rhoda responded and asked who it was. When Peter identified himself, she was so overjoyed that she left him standing there, and went to tell her friends that he was alive. Now comes the interesting factor: they didn't believe her. They had been praying all night, and yet they didn't believe that Peter had been delivered.

The story tells us about the effectiveness of prayer, but it also reminds us that many times we pray, not expecting anything to happen. It tells us also that many of us think of prayer as a last resort, a kind of last-ditch effort. When everything else fails we conclude, "guess there's nothing left to do but pray."

Incidentally, if you have problems with this story, you will have trouble with the entire biblical witness. Throughout scripture, God miraculously delivered from desperate circumstances: the Hebrew people crossing safely through the Red Sea; Daniel spending the night in the lion's den while the king who put him there spent a sleepless night; and on and on it goes. The Bible is full of stories of the miraculous intervention of God, and Peter's release from prison is one of them.

So, what would happen if we put prayer *first*? What if the Church believed that prayer is the greatest resource we have, not just praying, but praying from the perspective that we are acting as the Lord's intercessor.

Don't let the drama hide some sobering truths. Though the Christians were praying, they were obviously not offering bold prayers of intercession, and certainly there was not high expectation that their prayers would be answered. If there had been bold prayers—"in the name of Jesus, Lord deliver our leader; free him from Herod's evil forces "—Luke would have recorded it. Throughout his account of Acts, he gives careful attention to specific prayers and astounding answers. Had the story been otherwise, he would have wanted to use it as evidence that intercessory prayers were answered.

> What would happen if we put prayer *first*?

They prayed, yes, but probably the way too many of us pray, asking that Peter be sustained and strengthened. Though knowing what Herod intended to do, there was no bold, confident calling to the Lord for a miraculous intervention.

Note also that when God does exceedingly more than they ask, think, or even imagine, they can't believe it. "You're out of your mind," they told Rhoda when she tried to tell them that Peter was free and was at the door.

And maybe we should be "out of our minds" if our minds hinder us from boldly interceding.

Reflecting and Recording

1. Look at the way you have prayed over the past few months. Has your praying been primarily "a last-ditch effort?"

❖ ❖ ❖

2. Make some notes in your journal about the boldest prayer you can recall praying.

―――――――――――― During the Day ――――――――――――

Seek an opportunity to share with someone, other than persons with whom you are sharing this forty-day journey, about this venture. Tell them about what has been most meaningful to you thus far. Share in such a way they may want to talk about prayer in their life.

DAY 12

Some Distortions in Thinking About Intercession

I will praise you, Lord, with all my heart; before the "gods" I will sing your praise. I will bow down toward your holy temple and will praise your name for your unfailing love and your faithfulness, for you have so exalted your solemn decree that it surpasses your fame. When I called, you answered me; you greatly emboldened me

—Psalm 138:1–3

ONE OF OUR PROBLEMS IN PRACTICING INTERCESSION IS NOT *HOW* TO PRAY, but *what* to pray. We are reluctant in being specific in our intercession because we think, "who am I to tell God what to do?" You are God's child; I am God's child. God invites us to share what we think and what we feel, what we desire, and what we need.

For a long time in my personal prayer life, I was very hesitant to be bold and persistent in my praying. In reflection, this was due to two distortions in my thinking.

The first had to do with what I call "hedging my faith." My mind worked like this: If I am specific and bold and my prayers are not answered, what will that say about my faith? I was not willing for my faith to be questioned by me or by others. This mindset was at least in part the result of what I perceived as unanswered prayers. Such thinking wilts our willingness to pray boldly.

I discovered another distortion that was more subtle but severely limited my boldness in prayer. It was a false humility that made a great virtue of self-depreciation.

Very early in my ministry, I was uniquely blessed by having a marvelous elderly woman in the congregation who became a mentor in prayer. Because of her inspiration and guidance, I began to explore the broad expanses of prayer. She was also a person of significant financial resources, and because of her generosity, our small congregation was able to bring well-known spiritual leaders to our church for prayer conferences and retreats.

As a result, I was blessed to have personal contact with some folks whom I considered spiritual giants and great prayer warriors. I fell into the snare of comparing my prayer life to these "giants," measuring myself by their stature. You can imagine where I came out . . . a pygmy. Thus, my false humility and my self-depreciation.

> We are reluctant in being specific in our intercession because we think, "who am I to tell God what to do?"

For years, and sometimes even now, I find myself cowering back in prayer, thinking, "Who am I to pretend such confidence and claim such boldness in prayer?"

I have discovered that when my humility is authentic, I see my weakness and lack of boldness in proper light. I can acknowledge weakness, even my lack of faith, knowing that genuine humility is the one condition necessary to appropriate Holy Spirit power. It is when we know and confess that we are without power in relation to the issue about which we are praying, that we open the channels for the Holy Spirit's power to work.

In summary, these distortions I have described, and our general lack of faith in praying, are overcome by listening carefully, asking boldly, trusting completely, and knowing that whatever answers come to our praying, they will be a part of God's best plan for our lives and those for whom we pray.

Psalm 138, particularly the first three verses quoted above, has been a great source of encouragement for me. An earlier International Version of verse three has it, "When I called, you answered me; you made me bold and stouthearted."

Reflecting and Recording

1. Can you identify with the confession, 'hedging my faith'—unwilling to be specific and bold in praying, lest your faith would be questioned by others but also, by yourself if your prayers are not answered? How has this distortion been expressed in your experience?

✤ ✤ ✤

DAY 12: SOME DISTORTIONS IN THINKING ABOUT INTERCESSION

2. Comparing ourselves to others and measuring our spiritual maturity by comparison is a destructive pit into which it is easy to fall. Have you experienced this? Make some notes on your reflections.

✧ ✧ ✧

3. The author confessed a "false humility" and the practice of "self-depreciation" in his failure to "measure up," as he compared his spiritual stature to others. Focus on these two dynamics as you spend some time in self-examination.

✧ ✧ ✧

During the Day

Immersing ourselves in Scripture is one of the most important spiritual disciplines. We can't be persons of prayer without being persons of the word. Memorization of scripture is an important aspect of that discipline. Our first suggested memory verse was Hebrews 7:25 (Day 5). Did you memorize it?

Here is our second memory passage:

The Spirit helps us in our weakness. We do not know what we ought to pray for, but the Spirit himself intercedes for us through wordless groans. And he who searches our hearts knows the mind of the Spirit, because the Spirit intercedes for God's people in accordance with the will of God.

—ROMANS 8:26–27

Spend some time with it now, mark it in your Bible, or copy it in your journal, or copy it on a card you take it with you the next few days; read it over and over again—when you are stopped at traffic lights, waiting for an appointment, or even repeating it as a part of your blessing at meals—until you have committed it to memory.

DAY 13

Travailing: the Depth of Intercessory Prayer

The Spirit helps us in our weakness. We do not know what we ought to pray for, but the Spirit himself intercedes for us through wordless groans. And he who searches our hearts knows the mind of the Spirit, because the Spirit intercedes for God's people in accordance with the will of God.

—Romans 8:26–27

THE ACTS OF THE APOSTLES MIGHT WELL BE CALLED THE ACTS OF THE HOLY Spirit and two great truths stand out: First, where there is much prayer, there is vivid expression of the Holy Spirit; and second, where there is the vivid presence of the Holy Spirit, there is much praying. This dynamic relationship—prayer and the presence of the Holy—produces that which is beyond us, in fact, this is the source of miracles. One of the reasons we don't see more miracles is that we don't expect more miracles. Recalling the scripture passage from Day 11, Peter's friends were praying, but they were not expecting.

Paul's expression of the Holy Spirit's role in our praying—which is the memory passage we are presently working with—suggests the intimate connection between the Holy Spirit and intercession. As stated earlier, intercession is at the heart of our relationship to the Father, the risen and reigning Christ and to the Holy Spirit.

Two verses of scripture combine to give the picture. Romans 8:27 says, God, who searches the heart, knows what is the mind of the Spirit, because the Spirit intercedes for the saints according to the will of God. Put that with the exhilarating fact that Christ ever lives to make intercession for us and you have the dynamic work of the Trinity: Father, Son, and Holy Spirit. God searches our minds and the Holy Spirit becomes the intercessor of our hearts. As the Risen Lord, Jesus is the Great Intercessor, so the intercessions of the Holy Spirit and the Christ are one. As we abide in

Christ, which we are going to think more about in the days ahead, our intercession is one with the Holy Spirit and Christ, the Great Intercessor, in the throne room of heaven.

Look briefly now at a description of intercession that is present in both the Old and New Testaments. Paul gave expression to it in his prayer for the Galatians: "My little children, for whom I travail in birth again until Christ be formed in you" (Gal. 4:19, KJV). Note that Paul is "travailing" *again*. Those to whom he is writing are already Christian. Paul must be connecting his intense longing for them now (that Christ be formed in them) with the burning passion he had had for them to find freedom from the law that only faith in Christ could bring.

> One of the reasons we don't see more miracles is that we don't expect more miracles.

No word suggests the depth and intensity of intercessory prayer better than "travailing." No wonder Paul used the word. However, it is not unique to him. In the very first verses of the Bible, there is the description of the earth being formless and empty with darkness over the surface of the deep, and the Spirit of God hovering over the waters. Some translations say, the Spirit was "brooding over" and others, "moving upon the face of the waters."

The big idea is "birthing." The Spirit is birthing something, bringing forth life. As the different translations indicate, the Hebrew word, *rachaph*, used for "moving," literally means "to brood over." When you connect that with *brood* as a noun, you have that which has been bred or produced . . . as Webster defines it, "offspring" or "progeny." A mother hen has a *brood* of chicks, the little ones she has produced.

In his "song," which he recites in its entirety in Deuteronomy 32, Moses recounts Israel's history as God "birthing" a people. He describes the land and Abraham, the father of these "people of God," as being as barren as was the earth at creation. Then "like an eagle that stirs up the nest and hovers over its young" (v. 11), the Lord led Abraham. The Spirit "brooded" over Abraham and Sarah, releasing life and power, with the promise that they would conceive a child in their now barren years . . . a child who would be the beginning of the nation of God's own making. So 'birthing' is the work of the Holy Spirit. And 'birthing' is connected with 'travail.'

Dutch Sheets, who first called my attention to this birthing dynamic of intercession, reminds us that, "What the Holy Spirit was doing in Genesis when He 'brought forth' or 'gave birth to' the earth and the world is exactly what He wants to do though our prayers in bringing forth sons and daughters."[12]

Sheets is discussing the need for intercession for those who are not yet Christian, and how travailing is a good understanding of the kind of praying we should be doing for those we know and love who are not yet believers. His point is that the Holy Spirit wants to 'birth' these persons in the faith through us.

As indicated in the beginning of this discussion, Paul was "in travail *again*" for the Galatians. So he was connecting his intense longing that Christ be formed in them with his earlier burning passion for them to find freedom from the law and salvation that only faith in Christ could bring.

So travailing prayer is not just connected with the new birth of persons in the sense of conversion; it is also a form of intercession that releases the power of the Holy Spirit to give birth to something ongoing, redemptive, reconciling, and healing in persons.

Reflecting and Recording

1. Using your journal, describe one of the most difficult struggles of your life. Make enough notes to get that experience alive in your memory.

❖ ❖ ❖

2. Was prayer a part of that struggle? Would you call it 'travailing' prayer? Were you aware of the fact that the Holy Spirit intercedes for us? Did you sense the Holy Spirit present in your 'groans'?

❖ ❖ ❖

During the Day

Continue your focus on our memory passage. Bring this passage to awareness whenever you think of whatever problem or struggle you have.

DAY 14

God Needs You

You did not choose me, but I chose you and appointed you that you should go and bear fruit and that your fruit should abide; so that whatever you ask the Father in my name, he may give it to you.

—John 15:16, RSV

On day one of this journey, I shared the dramatic story from the Czech Republic. Eight women prayed for thirty years until the church was reopened and revived. Again, we register the claim that prayer is one of the greatest works that Christians are given to do.

Has it registered in you mind? God needs you! Is that a part of your awareness? Intercessory prayer is an essential aspect of our work as Christ Followers. Does that sound blasphemous—that the all-powerful, sovereign Lord of the universe needs us? Remember our claim: There are some things God either cannot or will not do until and unless people pray. In His sovereignty and power, God chose to order creation and all of life in such a way to include us in accomplishing His will. Elijah and Elijah's praying which we discussed earlier (Day 8) is a great demonstration of this.

Though it sounds so simple, it's a profound issue: *Prayer is God's idea.*

Think about it. Prayer raises some very tough questions. For instance, what about the sovereignty of God? Isn't God going to do whatever God wants to do whether we pray or not? Why should we pray for a person to be saved if that person doesn't want to be saved? Or what about healing? Does our praying make any difference? And what about our free will? Much of our praying is directed toward the needs, decisions, and directions of others. Do we expect our praying to impact their freedom? These are tough questions and many people do not pray because these questions paralyze them.

So it's important to register the fact that prayer is God's idea. I don't want to be irreverent, but all the questions and objections and contradictions surrounding prayer are God's problems—not mine—because God has commanded us to pray. I'm not suggesting that we don't have to wrestle with the problems and questions surrounding prayer—we do. I'm saying I don't have to *solve* those problems, or *answer* those questions, in order to pray. They're God's problem; God has commanded us to pray. Obviously, God needs us—why else would he command us to pray?

Again, *in no way does this assertion undermine or question the sovereignty of God*. God is all-powerful; God is in control. No question! The witness of scripture, however, and the experience of faithful followers is that God—in God's sovereignty—chooses persons to share in the Kingdom enterprise.

I have asked already something I ask often: *What if there are some things that God either cannot or will not do, until and unless people pray?* It's commonplace to think and affirm that God acts through persons. Acts of mercy and reconciliation, expressions of loving-kindness, deliberate righteous activity, justice deeds, performance that makes for peace—we see all of this as God's work through persons. We agree that God's will is accomplished through us.

Why is it such a long leap in our mind to think that as God is dependent upon our acting, so He is dependent upon our praying? Even a cursory review of the Bible confirms the fact that God's promises to act in our personal lives and in history is often connected with conditions to be met. The classic Old Testament challenge and promises are an obvious example; consider 2 Chronicles 7:14: "If my people who are called by my name will humble themselves and pray and seek my face and turn from their wicked ways [that's the condition, then comes the promise] then will I hear from Heaven and will forgive their sins and heal their land."

> Prayer is God's idea.

The classic example and promise in the New Testament is Jesus' promise, found in John 15:7: "If you abide in me and my words abide in you . . . that's the condition; if we meet the condition then Jesus says, ask whatever you wish, and it will be done for you."

Prayer is God's idea. Scripture witnesses to it constantly and the experience of the Christian community through the centuries is clear: There are some things God cannot or will not do until and unless God finds persons to pray. Meister Eckhart, the theologian, philosopher, and mystic, put the truth with extreme boldness: "God can as little do without us, as we without him."

God needs us. Again, this does not diminish the power and sovereignty of God; nor does it make God capricious. It simply affirms the relationship that is ours with the Creator Redeemer

God. It underscores the fact that God has given us the superlative opportunity to be active participants in the fulfillment of his Kingdom enterprise. John Baillie stated it succinctly: "Clearly we must not pray for any ends towards which it is wrong to labour, but likewise we must not labour for any end towards which it is wrong to pray."[13]

Prayer means no one of us can ever say, 'there is nothing I can do.' We can do what God calls us to do. We can partake in what God has designed as our channel through which He accomplishes what he wishes in the world: We can pray. So let's be done with the fear about questioning God's sovereignty and accept the fact that the Bible is full of principles that put responsibility upon us, which must be met to receive God's promises.

> God needs us. Again, this does not diminish the power and sovereignty of God; nor does it make God capricious.

Scripture offers abundant illustrations of this kind of intercession. In Isaiah 62:1, for example, the prophet Isaiah accepted this responsibility, and gave bold expression to it: "For Zion's sake I will not keep silent, for Jerusalem's sake I will not remain quiet, till her vindication shines out like the dawn, her salvation like a blazing torch." Here is a picture of intercession and *importunity*; Isaiah will not be kept silent, but will pester and intercede with God until Jerusalem has experienced a salvation that can be seen as clearly as a bright and burning torch. Isaiah is frustrated by God's delay in rebuilding Jerusalem's glory, as He had promised. To him, God appears stuck concerning His promise, so the prophet constantly speaks to God, reminding Him of His promises.

Other examples:

- God will bless Elijah and send rain on Israel, but Elijah must pray for it.
- If the chosen nation is to prosper, Samuel must plead for it.
- If the Jews are to be delivered, Daniel must intercede.
- God will bless Paul, and the nations shall be converted through him, but Paul must pray. And pray he did, without ceasing; his epistles show that he expected nothing except by asking for it.

This does not diminish God's grace, nor does it promote salvation by works. Think of it this way: the love of God is unconditional, but his favor and blessing require response and action on our part. God's promises are attached to governing principles that involve our active response.

Reflecting and Recording

1. Spend a bit of time reflecting on the fact that *God needs you.* Is this a new thought? Why do we have difficulty believing it?

❖ ❖ ❖

2. If you are in a sharing group, spend your remaining time thinking about your weekly meeting scheduled for today. Pray for the persons in your group. Review the guide for the meeting and make notes of any questions you want to ask, or issues you want to discuss.

❖ ❖ ❖

During the Day

Seek an occasion to share with a person (other than a person sharing your journey) what you are experiencing in this workbook journey.

Group Meeting for Week Two

Introduction

A part of your convenant for this forty-day journey was faithful attendance and sharing at the weekly gatherings. Your spiritual growth, in part, hinges upon your group participation, So share as openly as you can and listen to what others say. If you are attentive, you may pick up meaning beyond the surface of their words. Sensitive participation is crucial; responding immediately to the feelings you discern is also important.

At times, the group may need to focus its entire attention upon a particular individual; if some need or concern is expressed, the leader may ask the group to enter into a brief period of special prayer. But participants should not depend solely upon the leader for this kind of sensitivity. Even if you aren't the leader, don't hesitate to ask the group to join you in special prayer. This praying may be silent, or someone may wish to lead the group in a verbal prayer.

You have a contribution to make to the group. Even it you consider your thoughts or experiences trivial or unimportant, they may be exactly what another person needs to hear. Don't seek to be profound, but simply share your experience. Should you say something that is not well-received, or is misunderstood, don't be defensive or critical of yourself or others. Don't get diverted by overly scrutinizing your words and actions.

Sharing Together

Facilitator: Time may not permit you to use all the suggestions each week. Select what will most benefit your group. Be thoroughly familiar with these suggestions so that you can move through them selectively according to the direction in which the group is moving and according to the time available. Plan ahead, but do not hesitate to change your plans in response to the sharing taking place and the needs that emerge. The following is a broad outline to keep your group meeting moving, but be mindful that these are suggestions; be sensitive to the collective personality of your group and the direction of the Holy Spirit.

1. Open your time together with the leader offering a brief prayer of thanksgiving for the opportunity of sharing with the group, and petitions for openness in sharing and loving responses to one another.
2. Your were asked this week to share with someone, other than a person in the group, about your forty-day journey and what has been meaningful about thus far. Did any of you do that? Would a couple of you share that experience—particularly how people responded to your sharing?
3. On Days 9 and 10, we considered the Holy Spirit's place in the life of the church. Ask persons to turn to the notes they made during their reflecting and recording on those days, and spend ten to fifteen minutes responding to the questions:

   - How do you see the Holy Spirit at work?
   - What role does the Holy Spirit play in worship?
   - What role does the Holy Spirit play in decision making about program and mission? Leadership?
   - The ordering of your ongoing life together?

4. Invite two or three volunteers to share the boldest prayer they recall praying, what brought it about, what was the result of the praying.
5. On Day 12, the author (Maxie) spoke of some distortions in thinking about intercession. He confessed two limitations in his early life of prayer: one, what he called 'hedging my faith,' and two, a false humility that came from comparing his prayer life to that of others. Spend ten to fifteen minutes talking about how these problems, as well as others, have distorted and limited your practice of intercession.
6. On Day 13, we focused on 'travailing' as the depth of intercessory prayer. We were asked to reflect on the most difficult struggles of our life and whether prayer was a part of that struggle, whether we were aware of the Holy Spirit present in our "groans"? Invite two or three volunteers to share their experience.

7. Is there a question you have or an issue that was raised in the content this week that you would like to talk about? Spend as much time as you have and need for the group to respond. Remember, we don't have to have answers to all our questions, and we don't all have to agree. **Facilitator,** let the group discuss these issues and questions; you don't have to have the answers!

Praying Together

1. How are we faring with our memory work? Turn to Day 12, and let's read this week's memory passage, Romans 8:26–27 together as we begin our prayer time.
2. Praying corporately each week is a special ministry. Invite individuals to mention any special needs or concerns they wish to share with the entire group. A good pattern may be to ask for a period of prayer after each need is mentioned. This may be silent prayer, or one person may offer a brief two-or three-sentence verbal prayer.
3. Close your time by praying together the Lord's Prayer.

WEEK THREE
Life in Christ

DAY 15

The Indwelling Christ

Jesus answered: "Don't you know me, Philip, even after I have been among you such a long time? Anyone who has seen me has seen the Father. How can you say, 'Show us the Father'? Don't you believe that I am in the Father, and that the Father is in me? The words I say to you I do not speak on my own authority. Rather, it is the Father, living in me, who is doing his work. Believe me when I say that I am in the Father and the Father is in me; or at least believe on the evidence of the works themselves."

—John 14:9–11

THE APOSTLE PAUL'S TWO GREAT CONCEPTS OF THE CHRISTIAN FAITH WERE justification by grace through faith and the indwelling Christ. Protestant Christians have championed justification by grace through faith, but we have been slow in claiming the glorious possibility of *the indwelling Christ* . . . that we can live our lives *in Christ*.

Three times in John 14 Jesus makes the claim that he and the Father are one. He says it first when Thomas is mystified by Jesus' claim about going away "to prepare a place for us."

Thomas doesn't understand that: "We do not know where you are going. How can we know the way?" (v. 5) Jesus responds by making the claim that not only is he a way but *the* way. He is the one, visible expression of the invisible Father—this is the linchpin of the Christian faith. Jesus Christ is God present to us, and as we will presently discuss, *in us.*

Secondly, and within the same passage (John 14), Jesus makes the same claim in a different way when Philip begs, "Lord show us the Father, and we will be satisfied." Jesus chided him about his having been with him so long, and yet not knowing him. Then he pressed his claim. "I am in the Father and the Father is in me . . . the words that I say to you I do not speak on my own, but the Father who dwells in me does his works." (v. 8–10) Jesus' words and works are, in fact, the Father's.

> Jesus Christ is God present to us, and in us.

Thirdly, Jesus repeats the claim of the mutual indwelling of Father and Son in verse 20 with, "I am in the Father," and then adds the claim, 'you in me, and I in you.'

Jesus was not simply trying to prepare his disciples for his death, which was imminent, but for the glorious possibility that was going to follow. How they must have puzzled over his word: "I will not leave you desolate; I will come to you . . . and he who loves me will be loved by my father . . . and we (the father and I) . . . we will come to you and make our home in you" (John 14:18, 21, 23).

The Resurrection gave them hope and confirmed the victory of the Cross for our salvation; it wasn't until Pentecost, however, that the full meaning of the promise became clear . . . that indeed, Jesus would make his home in them. Can you imagine how baffling that word must have sounded? "The Father and I will come and make our home in you." It is on the foundation of that promise that Paul gives us dramatic expressions of his claims in his letter to the Ephesians:

- Verse 17: "that Christ may dwell in your heart through faith"
- Verse 18: "that you may be filled with all the fullness of God"

This is not isolated language for Paul; *"in Christ"* was a recurring theme. He used the phrase or its equivalent no less than 172 times in his epistles. His most vivid description of his own life in Christ was written to the *Galatians*: "I have been crucified with Christ; it is no longer I who live; but Christ who lives in me; and the life I now live in the flesh I live by faith in the Son of God, who loved me and gave himself for me" (Gal. 2:20, RSV). And in one of the boldest prayers ever prayed,

DAY 15: THE INDWELLING CHRIST

Paul interceded "that through faith Christ may dwell in your hearts in love . . . so may you attain to fullness of being, the fullness of God Himself" (Eph. 3:17, 19, NEB).

The distilled meaning of these references is that God's mysterious secret which has been hidden and which persons through the ages had sought to probe and decipher, has now been revealed. That mystery is Christ: Christ **in you.**

Reflecting and Recording

1. Spend a few minutes examining your Christian experience in relation to Paul's two great concepts of the Christian faith. When and how did you claim that you were "justified by grace through faith"? Have you heard that language in teaching and preaching? Do you use that language in conversation about the Christian faith?

✧ ✧ ✧

2. What about the indwelling Christ? Have you been aware of this possibility—that Christ desires to "abide" in you? Has this been a part of your understanding and experience?

✧ ✧ ✧

3. Reflect on this statement: *Jesus Christ is God present to us and in us.* What is the difference between Christ being present to us and in us? Has this been a part of your thinking about Christ in the past? What does Christ mean when he says, "We (the Father and I) will make our home in you"?

During the Day

I am the vine itself; you are the branches. It is the man who shares my life and whose life I share who proves fruitful. For the plain fact is that apart from me you can do nothing at all.

—John 15:5, Phillips

Read this verse three or four times, and take it with you as your memorization passage for this week.

DAY 16

The Great Mystery of the Christian Faith

Now I rejoice in what I am suffering for you, and I fill up in my flesh what is still lacking in regard to Christ's afflictions, for the sake of his body, which is the church. I have become its servant by the commission God gave me to present to you the word of God in its fullness—the mystery that has been kept hidden for ages and generations, but is now disclosed to the Lord's people. To them God has chosen to make known among the Gentiles the glorious riches of this mystery, which is Christ in you, the hope of glory. He is the one we proclaim, admonishing and teaching everyone with all wisdom, so that we may present everyone fully mature in Christ. To this end I strenuously contend with all the energy Christ so powerfully works in me.

—Colossians 1:24–29

In this passage, Paul gave witness to Christ's presence within, which he called the great mystery of the Christian faith. At least three truths are evident in the passage.

The first truth is the *Incarnation: God has come to us in Jesus Christ.* Earlier in this first chapter of his Letter to the Colossians, Paul encapsulated the essence of God's saving work in Jesus: "He has rescued us from the power of darkness and transferred us into the kingdom of his beloved Son, in whom we ever have redemption, the forgiveness of sins" (Col. 1:13–14). Having sounded that astounding good news, Paul felt it wise to tell us who this Son really is, into whose kingdom we have been brought:

> The Son is the image of the invisible God, the firstborn over all creation. For in him all things were created: things in heaven and on earth, visible and invisible, whether thrones or powers or rulers or authorities; all things have been created through him and for him. He is before all things, and in him all things hold together. And he is the head of the body, the church; he is the beginning and the firstborn from among the dead, so that in everything he might have the supremacy. For God was pleased to have all his fullness dwell in him, and through him to

reconcile to himself all things, whether things on earth or things in heaven, by making peace through his blood, shed on the cross."—Col. 1:15–20

In proclaiming this gospel, Paul underscores the importance of the Incarnation. Christ is the mystery of God and the kingdom now revealed. He is our salvation.

The second truth Paul proclaims and underscores is Christ's ongoing presence in the life of the believer. He stated it this way: "To this end I strenuously contend with all the energy Christ so powerfully works in me" (v. 29).

The presence of a new power (Christ's energy) within is what enables us to break away from our old life. We turn from the old through repentance and are released to the new through forgiveness.

The third truth is the goal of the gospel's work in our life—that we might be presented "mature in Christ" (NRSV). So Christ is an immediate—but also an ongoing—transforming power over our character. In the kingdom of God's dear Son, we have superhuman power over the evils of this present age.

> The presence of God in Jesus Christ is not to be experienced only on occasion; rather, the indwelling Christ is to become the shaping power of our lives.

In *The Workbook on Lessons From the Saints,* I discussed the ten characteristics I discovered in my discipline of keeping company with the saints. One of them was *Jesus was alive in their experience.* A careful reading of scripture and the writings of the saints make it clear: The presence of God in Jesus Christ is not to be experienced only on occasion; rather, the indwelling Christ is to become the shaping power of our lives. When Jesus used words like "in me you may have peace" (John 16:33), the "in me" language is probably connected with his metaphor of the vine and the branches. So it is not a matter of an experience of Christ now and then, but the indwelling Christ as an ongoing reality, that becomes the shaping power of our lives.

In *Lessons From the Saints,* I shared the story of Bill, a friend whose witness illustrates this shaping power of Christ. He says that while he can't remember when he became a Christian, he does remember and talks glowingly about an eight-week study of *Alive in Christ,* which he and his wife shared with four other couples. In his words, "Christ came alive in me." The study had taken place over ten years before. In his e-mail in which he was sharing his witness, he wanted me to hear the good news of a Chinese man who had that day professed his faith in Christ.

Bill and his wife had "adopted" this man, a student at a local university simply to show hospitality and, of course, in the hopes of sharing a Christian witness. The fellow was not open to Christianity; in fact, he was hostile to it. But after a year of friendship with Bill and Sue, he not only became open to the gospel, he embraced it and claimed its saving power. In Bill's words, "It was Christ in us and through us, shaping our lives in love and concern for the stranger in our midst, that won this person."[14]

Reflecting and Recording

1. Spend a few minutes pondering this claim: *The presence of God in Jesus Christ is not to be experienced only on occasion; rather, the indwelling Christ is to become the shaping power of our lives.* Do you believe this is true? How does it happen?

✣ ✣ ✣

2. To what degree and in what way is the indwelling Christ shaping your life? Make some notes.

✣ ✣ ✣

3. Paul made the claim that the indwelling Christ "powerfully works in me." In your journal, write the names of two or three people you know in whom you would say Christ is working powerfully.

✣ ✣ ✣

4. Think about these persons for a few minutes. What characterized their lives? What about them causes you to think that Christ is working powerfully in them? What do they have that is missing in your life, or that you would like to have more of?

THE INTERCESSORY LIFE

❖ ❖ ❖

During the Day

There is a form of prayer we call 'arrow prayers' . . . brief, spontaneous expressions of desires addressed to God. As you move through this and coming days, practice the discipline of arrow prayer with this: "Lord, give me the grace to be completely yours."

DAY 17

The Secret

I am glad when I suffer for you in my body, for I am participating in the sufferings of Christ that continue for his body, the church. God has given me the responsibility of serving his church by proclaiming his entire message to you. This message was kept secret for centuries and generations past, but now it has been revealed to God's people. For God wanted them to know that the riches and glory of Christ are for you Gentiles, too. And this is the secret: Christ lives in you. This gives you assurance of sharing his glory.

—Colossians 1:24–27, NLT

Off and on for thirty years, my morning ritual has included a word to myself: "Maxie, the secret is simply this, Christ in you, yes, Christ in you, bringing with him the hope of all the glorious things to come." Sometimes I speak it aloud, sometimes I simply register it in my awareness. Sometimes I make it a liturgy, repeating it over and over again to a breathing in-breathing out exercise.

As we noted on Day 15, Paul's understanding of the Christian faith revolved around two basic concepts: one, justification by grace through faith, and two, a person *in Christ*. We beome Christian by being justified by grace through faith. We live the Christian life by abiding in Christ.

It is interesting that in his writing, Paul does not tell us about his Damascus Road experience in descriptive detail; Luke actually records the details of that dramatic event in the Acts of the Apostles. Nor does Paul write about being struck down by a blinding light and hearing the voice of Christ; rather, he talks about the meaning of that experience. When we read his testimony, we can feel his overflowing joy: "I have been crucified with Christ; it is no longer I who live, but Christ who lives in me; and the life I now live in the flesh I live by faith in the Son of God, who loved me and gave himself for me" (Gal. 2:20).

So we talk about becoming Christian using terms like *accepting* Christ, *inviting* Christ into our lives, *receiving* Christ as Savior, being *born again* by allowing Christ to be born in us. Whatever the language, the faith and experience is that as we confess our sins, we are forgiven, justified by Christ and enter into a new relationship with God who then lives in us through the power of the Holy Spirit as the indwelling Christ.

> Too often we have a faith that seeks, but not a faith that rests.

Hudson Taylor, the great missionary and founder of the China Inland Mission, had a favorite expression for our life in Christ; he called it "the *exchanged* life." This was his 'spiritual secret' and he embodied the truth.

In 1869, he experienced a "dark night of the soul." His eight-year-old daughter had died. The intense political unrest and the responsibility he carried for the missionaries and the movement itself weighted him down. He wrote his mother, mourning about following Jesus at such a distance and learning so slowly to imitate "my precious Master." He continued: "I cannot tell you how I am buffeted sometimes by temptations. I never knew how bad a heart I have . . . Often I am tempted to think that one so full of sin cannot be a child of God at all . . . Pray that the Lord will keep me from sin, will sanctify me wholly, will use me more largely in his service."[15]

Six months later, Taylor's prayer was answered through a letter he received from a fellow missionary John Macarthy, who shared what he had discovered about the life of holiness: "His life, His death, His work, He Himself as revealed to us in the Word, to be the subject of your constant thoughts. Not a striving to have faith . . . but looking off to the Faithful One seems all we need; a resting in the Loved One entirely, for time and for eternity."[16]

When Hudson Taylor read those words on Saturday September 4, 1869, in the little mission station at Chin-kiang, the scales fell off his eyes and he perceived his union with Christ as never before. He wrote his sister, describing what had happened. This is part of what he said:

"Ah, there is rest!" I thought. I have striven in vain to rest in Him. I'll strive no more. For has not He promised to abide with me—never to leave me, never to fail me? And, . . . He never will.

"I am dead and buried with Christ—ay, and risen too! And now Christ lives in me, and "the life I now live in the flesh I live by the faith of he Son of God, who loved me and gave himself for me."[17]

To Macarthy's point: In the pursuit of holiness, too often we have a faith that seeks, but not a faith that rests, thus the joyful confidence of abiding in Christ eludes us. Our faith can be transformed by thinking of all that Jesus *is* and all He *is for* us.

Reflecting and Recording

1. Spend some time thinking about the distinction between seeking faith and resting faith. Should the time come, and what would that time be like, when we move from seeking faith to resting faith? Have you made that move in your life?

✧ ✧ ✧

During the Day

Write the following statement on a piece of paper, filling in the blank with your name:

_____, the secret is simply this, Christ in you, yes Christ in you; bringing with him the hope of all the glorious things to come.

Carry this statement with you—in your Bible, or journal, or put it on your bathroom mirror or the dashboard of your car, or on the kitchen table where you will see it and claim it often.

DAY 18

The Vine and the Branches

I am the true vine, and my Father is the gardener. He cuts off every branch in me that bears no fruit, while every branch that does bear fruit he prunes so that it will be even more fruitful.

—John 15:1–2

On day 15, we began our consideration of Paul's understanding of the indwelling Christ as one of his two primary concepts of the Christian faith. But it is not only Paul who uses that language. In John 15, Jesus' allegory of the vine and the branches tells us who the Father is, and who Jesus himself is in relation to the Father.

From there, Jesus tells us who we are in relation to Him: "I am the vine itself; you are the branches. It is the man who shares my life and whose life I share who proves fruitful. For the plain fact is that apart from me you can do nothing at all" (John 15:1–5, Phillips).

The dynamic of the Christian life is abiding in Christ. Each of us is connected to Jesus as a branch is connected to the vine. Our story as Christ followers is inextricably linked with the story of Jesus. As we abide in Christ, prayer becomes our life and our life becomes our prayer. It is what we mean when we talk about *an intercessory life.* This is a breathtaking truth. To claim it and make it real is our role in the drama of creation and redemption. We become one with Christ, thus becoming "little Christs."

C.S. Lewis expressed it boldly: "The church exists for nothing else but to draw men into Christ, to make them little Christs. If they are not doing that, all the cathedrals, clergy, missions, sermons, even the Bible itself, are simply a waste of time. God became Man for no other purpose. It is even doubtful . . . whether the whole universe was created for any other purpose. It says in the Bible that the whole universe was made for Christ and that everything is to be gathered together in Him."[18]

Going back to Jesus' word—*I am the vine, you are the branches*—we must remember that there is always a distinction between the vine and the branches. The branches do not sustain the vain; the vine sustains the branches. But we need to claim this exhilarating truth: *The vine cannot express itself*

DAY 18: THE VINE AND THE BRANCHES

except through the branches. Christ is dependent upon us for the expression of his life in the world, and that is an intercessory life.

> As we abide in Christ, prayer becomes our life and our life becomes our prayer.

Again, unfathomable mystery is here, but mystery we can claim boldly as Christians. We have been given the privilege of being connected intimately to God, primarily through our abiding in Christ. In the same way that the Father and the Son are connected with one another, so we are connected with the Son by the work of the Holy Spirit. "He who unites himself with the Lord is one with him in spirit" (1 Cor. 6:17). There is unspeakable joy in this privilege, but there is also the power to be used by God as instruments of making all persons his dwelling place, and all creation showing his glory. Intercession is one of the chief channels and means of grace through which the Father does his work in the world. The awesome fact is that intercession, unceasing intercession, opens the doors of heaven for the Father's blessings to flow and for persons to become partakers of those blessings. The intercession of God's people is a huge instrument in the coming of God's Kingdom and the doing of God's will on earth as it is in heaven (Matt. 6:10).

Here we make the claim that is the primary theme of this book: Intercession is a form of prayer, but more, it is the life style of Christ followers. We are to live intercessory lives.

—————————————— Reflecting and Recording ——————————————

1. Spend a bit of time reflecting on the statement of C.S. Lewis: "The Church exists for nothing else but to draw men into Christ, to make them little Christs." Is this a new thought? Do you believe it? What questions does it raise?

✤ ✤ ✤

—————————————— During the Day ——————————————

Consider your memory verse throughout the day. Remember, the vine cannot express itself except through the branches.

DAY 19

Greater Works Will You Do

Believe me when I say that I am in the Father and the Father is in me; or at least believe on the evidence of the works themselves. Very truly I tell you, whoever believes in me will do the works I have been doing, and they will do even greater things than these, because I am going to the Father. And I will do whatever you ask in my name, so that the Father may be glorified in the Son. You may ask me for anything in my name, and I will do it.

—John 14:11–14

It is challenging to note that in the midst of his claim to his disciples that he and the Father would make his home in them (John 14), Jesus made one of his most breathtaking statements: "the one who has faith in me will do greater works than these, because I am going to the Father" (v. 12). Now here is another foundational truth for our understanding of intercessory prayer and an intercessory life: After Jesus' ascension to the Father, he will continue to do his work through his disciples.

One of the most challenging facts flowing out of Jesus' conversation about his death, resurrection, and "making his home in us," is that we are partners with Christ in intercession. If he is the Great Intercessor, could it be that intercession is a big part of the "greater works than I have done will you do because I go to the Father" that Jesus was talking about?

When I was leaving Christ Church to become the President of Asbury Seminary, one of the gifts they gave me was an enlarged reproduction of one of Charles Schulz's "Peanuts" cartoons. They knew my fondness for his playful but profound expressions of theology, and I used them often in sermon illustrations.

Charlie Brown is the central character in the cartoons. He is always the 'loser'—his friends take advantage of him, tease him mercilessly, and give him no affirmation. The cartoon given to me, shows Charlie Brown leaping with joy, dancing, and cutting cartwheels as he comes to the door of his home shouting, "I hit a homerun in the ninth inning! I was the hero!" His sister, Sally, takes all the joy out of his celebration with her incredulous, "YOU?"

Sometimes people do that to us . . . questioning any accomplishment or giftedness. But that is not our problem in living the Christian life—we, not others, are the problem when we do not claim the promise of Jesus to do "greater works."

What did Jesus say he would do when he went to the Father? He said he would send the Holy Spirit. And what would the Holy Spirit do? Give us "power when the Holy Spirit comes upon you" (Acts 1:8).

In discussing intercession in the New Testament church in Week Two, we made the connection between the Holy Spirit and intercession.

The Acts of the Apostles might well be called the Acts of the Holy Spirit, as two great truths stand out: where there is much prayer, there is the vivid presence of the Holy Spirit; where there is the vivid presence of the Holy Spirit, there is much praying. This dynamic relationship—prayer and the presence of the Holy Spirit—produces that which is beyond us; in fact, this is the source of miracles. One of the reasons we don't see more miracles is that we don't expect more miracles.

> What is true of the empowerment by the Holy Spirit is also true in our actions.

What is true of the empowerment by the Holy Spirit—through our praying—is also true in our actions. In describing the church without dependence on the Holy Spirit, Samuel Chadwick said, "the Church always fails at the the point of self-confidence."[19] What is true of the church is true of us as individuals. We don't do "greater things than these" because we don't believe we can, and we can't get our attention off our own self-resources; our self-confidence is a barrier to dependence on the Holy Spirit.

Some time ago, one of our Asbury graduates, Jeanine Brabon, sent me a gift that I treasure—a wood carving of praying hands. I keep it in my study as a reminder that I am a partner with Christ in the demanding and thrilling call to intercession.

Jeanine is a missionary, working in Medellin, Columbia. Her primary assignment is as an Old Testament professor in the seminary there, but her most exciting work is connected with the Bellavista prison. In 2009, the World Methodist Council gave her the World Methodist Peace

Award for her work in this prison and for reconciliation in that war-ravaged nation. There, along with others, a mighty Holy Spirit-empowered work is being accomplished.

Bellavista has been one of the worst prisons in all of Latin and South America. It was built to house 1,500 inmates. Five thousand were packed into it like bundles of human flesh. Until a few years ago, it was a hell-pit of violence and inhumanity—prisoners raping one another; heads cut off and kicked about like soccer balls; men hung up and quartered like hogs at the market; fifty homicides each month. Then, it happened.

Oscar Osorio envisioned God wrapping the prison in his hands, and received divine orders to raise white flags outside the cell blocks where prayer was taking place. Prayer swept the prison and within six years, Christian conversion began to replace homicide. Where there had been fifty homicides per month, there has been only one per year since 1990 when Oscar Osorio and a band of Christians had their vision and responded. A secular jurist reported that violence in the prison diminished 90 percent. The warden and everyone recognized the power behind the transformation; there were prayer groups in every cell block.[20]

> "There is nothing struck by disaster or devastated by sin that cannot be transformed by the Master's hands."
> —Jeanine Brabon, missionary

My praying hands were carved by Carlos Velasquez, who was a prisoner in Bellavista and converted as a result of the baptism of that prison in prayer and a radical dependence upon the Holy Spirit. In Carlos's mind, the hands are the hands of Jesus. When you look at them, on the left one you can see a black streak left by the lightning that struck the tree out of which it was carved.

In her note to me, with this gift, Jeanine wrote, "There is nothing struck by disaster or devastated by sin that cannot be transformed by the Master's hands." Then she added, "The hands that carved these praying hands once processed cocaine for one of Colombia's biggest drug lords. Praise God. With Him, nothing is impossible!"

Jeanine, Carlos, and Oscar Osorio have accepted Jesus' promise, "Greater things than I have done will you do." They are living *in Christ*.

Reflecting and Recording

1. To ponder, according to Webster, is to "think deeply about," "to consider carefully." It is not all of, but is a part of, reflecting. Spend a bit of time pondering Jesus' promise, "*Greater things than I have done will you do.*"
2. Then ask yourself: *Do I believe that? To what degree, or in what way do I believe it? What do my actions and attitudes say about whether and how I believe it?*

✥ ✥ ✥

During the Day

Our ongoing temptation is to think we can manage our own lives and do what we set our minds to; it is the illusion of self-sufficiency, and is the place where Satan can do his most effective work. As you move throughout the day, when thoughts of self-sufficiency begin to take shape, think of that part of your memory verse where Jesus says, "Apart from me you can do nothing at all."

DAY 20

A Simple Practice With Profound Meaning

*And we all, who with unveiled faces contemplate the Lord's glory,
are being transformed into his image with ever-increasing glory,
which comes from the Lord, who is the Spirit.*

—2 Corinthians 3:18

Return to Paul's two great concepts of the Christian faith: justification by grace through faith and the indwelling Christ. Could it be that we have ignored the notion of the indwelling Christ and Jesus' promise that he would dwell in us because we simply don't believe it? Is it too radical for us to own for ourselves? This is a breathtaking truth . . . that Christ will dwell in us, that we can live our lives in Christ. Claiming this possibility and making it real, we become one with Christ, thus becoming "little Christs."

If Christ is the Great Intercessor, an intercessory life calls us to become more and more like Christ—and that should not be a foreign idea. Wherever the story of Jesus is known, most persons would say that to be like Jesus is the greatest possible human attainment. Though we may be full of excuses/reasons for not being like Jesus, most of us would want to be and would think that being like him would be the greatest thing that could happen in our lives. Yet, our conclusion is, "impossible . . . it could never be."

In the scripture reference above, the Apostle Paul challenges us in this thought that being like Christ is impossible. We *all*, Paul says . . . not a person now and then, not persons in rare circumstances with exceptional opportunities, but *all* Christians have that possible destiny of being transformed into Christ's image. As we stated previously, this is a dominant conviction of Paul. A "person *in Christ*" was a recurring theme in his sharing about the Christian faith and way. This is the way he talked about the Christian life.

Jesus' metaphor of the vine and the branches is one of the three or four scripture passages that have impacted my life the most:

DAY 20: A SIMPLE PRACTICE WITH PROFOUND MEANING

I am the true vine, and my Father is the gardener. He cuts off every branch in me that bears no fruit, while every branch that does bear fruit he prunes so that it will be even more fruitful. You are already clean because of the word I have spoken to you. Remain in me, and I will remain in you. No branch can bear fruit by itself; it must remain in the vine. Neither can you bear fruit unless you remain in me. I am the vine; you are the branches. If a man remains in me and I in him, he will bear much fruit; apart from me you can do nothing.—John 15:1-5

This promise of Jesus led me to study Paul's understanding of the Christian life as "abiding in Christ." Out of that study and my commitment to make that the goal of my life has emerged my definition of spiritual formation: "That dynamic process of receiving through faith and appropriating through commitment, discipline, and action, the living Christ into our own life to the end that our life will conform to and manifest the reality of Christ's presence in the world."

> If Christ is the Great Intercessor, an intercessory life calls us to become more and more like Christ—and that should not be a foreign idea.

For many years, I have sought to practice disciplines that enhance my *recognizing and cultivating awareness of the indwelling Christ*. I have not paid enough attention to the simplest way of becoming like Christ; Marcus Dods brought this to my attention by suggesting that when Paul made his claim about the possibility of our being transformed from one degree of glory to another, he must have been thinking about Moses.

When Moses descended Mount Sinai, after having been with God and having received the Ten Commandments, his face was so radiant that the Israelites were afraid to come near him. They knew the glory of God was being reflected through Moses.

After Moses delivered the Ten Commandments, "he put a veil over his face. But whenever he entered the Lord's presence to speak with him, he removed the veil until he came out. And when he came out and told the Israelites what he had been commanded, they saw that his face was radiant. Then Moses would put the veil back over his face until he went in to speak with the Lord" (Ex. 34:33–35).

Dods suggests that Moses:

> . . . knew that the glory was only on the skin of his face, and that of course it would pass away. It was a superficial shining. And accordingly, he put a veil over his face, that the children of Israel

might not see it dying out from minute to minute and from hour to hour, because he knew these Israelites thoroughly, and he knew that when they saw the glory dying out they would say, 'God has forsaken Moses. We need not attend to him any more. His authority is gone, and the glory of God's presence has passed from him.' So Moses wore the veil that they might not see the glory dying out. But when he was called back to he presence of God he took off the veil and received a new access of glory on his face, and thus went 'from glory to glory.'[21]

How have we missed it, and why do we make it so complicated? The simple way of becoming like Christ to which I am giving more attention is spending time in Christ's presence with unveiled face, believing that as I stand before Christ, think of him, reflect on his character, act as I think he would act, he confers his glory to me. Granted, this is a reflected glory, but what Paul is saying to us is that we are, in fact, changed from glory to glory into the very image of Christ.

Reflecting and Recording

The following is a part of Paul's prayer for the Christians in Ephesus. Believing scripture as I do, I believe it is a prayer for all Christians:

> I pray that out of his glorious riches he may strengthen you with power through his Spirit in your inner being, so that Christ may dwell in your hearts through faith. (Eph. 3:16–17)

Write it in your own words in your journal as a personal prayer for yourself.

❖ ❖ ❖

Now pray it three or four times before you leave this period of Reflecting and Recording.

❖ ❖ ❖

During the Day

You know the sense of this prayer now. Find four or five occasions during the day to pray it: while driving, waiting for an appointment, or as a part of your blessing at mealtime.

DAY 21

The Holy Spirit Joins Us to the Risen Lord

I pray that out of his glorious riches he may strengthen you with power through his Spirit in your inner being, so that Christ may dwell in your hearts through faith. And I pray that you, being rooted and established in love, may have power, together with all the saints, to grasp how wide and long and high and deep is the love of Christ, and to know this love that surpasses knowledge— that you may be filled to the measure of all the fullness of God.

—Ephesians 3:16–19

On Day 19, I shared about Carlos, who was converted in the Bellavista Prison. His carving of Jesus' praying hands is a treasured gift and an ongoing inspiration. He spent three weeks on our Asbury Seminary campus a few years ago, carving a larger than life figure of Jesus as the "Good Shepherd," with a lamb over his shoulder. That carving is in the lobby of the Student Commons at the seminary.

Carlos not only witnesses with his art, he travels in this country and throughout Latin and South America, witnessing to the Lord of Bellavista as the Lord of his life. He will tell you that the Holy Spirit, through the dynamic of prayer, transformed his life and the life of that hellish prison. He will also tell you that he is seeking to live and love like Jesus. He not only practices intercessory prayer, he seeks to live an intercessory life.

Carlos is a living witness to a claim I want to solidify in your mind: *The New Testament makes it clear there is no awareness of the presence of the Risen Christ to us or in us except through the Holy Spirit, and there can be no convincing validation of the claim that one has the Holy Spirit unless this is accompanied by signs of Jesus' presence.* The Holy Spirit joins us to the risen Lord, and this relationship produces a life set apart for him. We may say it either way: the Holy Spirit is present in us as the indwelling Christ or Christ is present in us as the Holy Spirit.

These truths are present in the Paul's prayer for the Christians in Ephesus . . . *and for all Christians!* The Holy Spirit works in our inner being to join us to the risen Lord, who lives in us. The signs of his presence provide the essential witness of our commitment. So, as we contended yesterday, it is absolutely crucial that we pay attention to Christ, spending time in his presence.

For me, the most beautiful and challenging picture of Jesus in Scripture is Paul's description of him in his letter to the Phillippians:

> Let this mind be in you, which was also in Christ Jesus:
> Who, being in the form of God,
>   thought it not robbery to be equal with God:
> But made himself of no reputation,
>   and took upon him the form of a servant,
>   and was made in the likeness of men:
> And being found in fashion as a man,
>   he humbled himself, and became obedient unto death,
>   even the death of the cross.
> Wherefore God also hath highly exalted him,
>   and given him a name which is above every name:
> That at the name of Jesus every knee should bow,
>   of things in heaven, and things in earth,
>   and things under the earth;
> And that every tongue should confess that Jesus Christ is Lord,
>   to the glory of God the Father."—Phil. 2:5–11, KJV

> We may say it either way: the Holy Spirit is present in us as the indwelling Christ or Christ is present in us as the Holy Spirit.

Poverty of spirit is the foundation of the house of spiritual character. There is a sense in which Jesus surrendered "being equal with God," he took on "the likeness of men," humbled himself and became obedient. Jesus' beatitudes in the Sermon on the Mount contain the kernel of his teaching; it is also clear that these beatitudes essentially describe Jesus' character. He lived these beatitudes. I believe it is significant that the first one is in total harmony with Paul's picture of Jesus: "Blessed are the poor in spirit, for theirs is the kingdom of heaven" (Matt. 5:3).

DAY 21: THE HOLY SPIRIT JOINS US TO THE RISEN LORD

An intercessory life calls us to become more and more like Christ. And we want that . . . we want to be like Christ, so we say. Yet, we keep thinking it is not possible. Paul challenges us here. We reflected on his claim the past couple of days: "And we all, who with unveiled faces contemplate the Lord's glory, are being transformed into his image with ever-increasing glory, which comes from the Lord, who is the Spirit" (2 Cor. 3:18). As we recognize and cultivate Christ's indwelling presence, we are shaped into his likeness, and we reflect his presence in the world.

Reflecting and Recording

Reflect and respond in your mind and heart to these questions as you examine your "likeness to Christ."

- Do you love?
- Are you kind and compassionate?
- Is your heart breaking for the brokenness of the world?
- Do you seek to empty yourself so there is more room for Jesus?
- Do you care for others more than for yourself?

✣ ✣ ✣

During the Day

Be attentive to opportunities to act like Jesus. Perform at least two actions that you would consider 'Jesus Acts.'

Group Meeting for Week Three

Introduction

Feedback and follow-up are key ingredients for a Christian fellowship. Feedback keeps the group dynamic working positively for all participants. Follow-up expresses Christian concern and ministry.

The leader is the one primarily responsible for feedback and can elicit it by encouraging all members to share their feelings about how the group is functioning. Listening is crucial. When we listen to another, we are saying, "You are important. I value you. Being sure we understand what another is saying is also crucial. We often mishear, so, don't hesitate to ask, "Do I hear you saying _____?" If a couple of persons in a group listen and give feedback in this fashion, they can set the tone for the entire group.

Follow-up is the function of everyone. If we listen to what others say, we will discover needs and concerns beneath the surface, situations that deserve special prayer and attention. Make notes of these as the group shares. Follow up during the week with a telephone call, an encouraging note, or maybe a personal visit. The distinguishing quality of Christian fellowship is caring in action. Ideally our caring should be so evident that others notice and remark, "My, how those Christians love one another!" Saint Augustine said, "All our good and all our evil certainly lies in the character of our actions. As they are, so are we; for we are the tree, and they the fruit, and, therefore, they prove what each one is."[22] So, be attentive and follow up with each group member.

Sharing Together

Hopefully by this time, individuals are beginning to feel safe in the group and perhaps more willing to share. Still, there is no place for pressure. Be sensitive to those who are slow to share. Coax them gently, remembering that every person is a gift to the group.

You may want to consider the following suggestions to keep the group meeting moving along at a comfortable pace, always being mindful of the group's collective personality:

GROUP MEETING FOR WEEK THREE

1. There is nothing quite like singing to bring a body together and to flavor fellowship and sharing. This week we have focused on Jesus as a saving and abiding presence. Sing a hymn or chorus most everyone will know: "Jesus Loves Me," "O How I Love Jesus," "Amazing Grace," etc.
2. Read together Colossians 1:24–29, which is printed at the beginning of Day 16. Have either a facilitator or a volunteer offer a brief prayer of thanksgiving and request for freedom and honesty in sharing.
3. Invite a couple of volunteers to share their "justification by grace through faith" experience (the time and/or process of professing their faith in Christ and accepting him as Savior and Lord).
4. On Day 4 of our forty-day journey, we considered the fact that the faith that was necessary in our accepting Christ for salvation is the same faith we need to exercise in our praying. Spend a few minutes discussing this in light of the experiences of faith that have been shared.
5. The big claim of the gospel that we have considered this week is that "the presence of God is Jesus Christ is not to be experienced only on occasion, the indwelling Christ is to become the shaping power of our lives." Most of your time should be spent responding to this claim. Use the following questions to help guide the discussion:

   - Is the possibility that we can live our lives *in Christ* a new idea? Have you heard it preached and taught very much?
   - How aware have you been that Christ desires to abide in you and you to abide in him?
   - What experience have you had of Christ dwelling "in your heart through faith"?
   - What do you think Jesus means when he says, "We (the Father and I) will make our home in you"?

6. Seek to focus your conversation for a few minutes by responding to the question: What is the difference between Christ being present *to us* and present *in us*?
7. Spend a few minutes discussing the difference between "seeking" and "resting" faith. Invite persons to indentify whether they live in the mode of "seeking" or "resting" faith.
8. Spend the balance of you discussion time responding to C.S. Lewis's claim, "The church exists for nothing else but to draw men into Christ to make them little Christs."

Praying Together

William Law said the following about spiritual disciplines: "He who has learned to pray has learned the greatest secret of a holy and happy life."

1. Invite three or four people to pray aloud Paul's prayer for the Ephesians as they rewrote it during the Reflecting and Recording on Day 20.
2. Invite the group to share any prayer concerns they have. After each expression of concern, ask a volunteer to offer a brief prayer.
3. Close your time by praying aloud together this prayer:

Dear Jesus, be present in me in a powerful way as I move though the coming days. Possess my mind, my heart, my will. Let no word cross my lips that is not your word. Let no thoughts be cultivated that are not your thoughts. Let no deeds be done that are not an expression of your love and concern. May your presence be real to me in that others will no longer see me but you, Lord Jesus. may I be cheered by your presence and move through these coming days with no hint of anxiety, so that your peace may flow from my life, Amen.

WEEK FOUR
An Intercessory Life

DAY 22

Responsible *To* or *For* Christ

He will reply, "I tell you the truth, whatever you did not do for one of the least of these, you did not do for me."

—Matthew 25:45

I PREACHED IN A SERIES OF WORSHIP SERVICES AT A CHURCH IN A UNIVERSITY town. After the last service, a young man kept hanging around; I knew he wanted to talk, yet he was shy, and other people kept greeting me. Finally I was able to give him my full attention.

He began by saying he could not leave the meeting without speaking to me. He spoke haltingly, almost in a stutter, but as he began to talk his eyes sparkled and his speech became clearer, and more fluent. He reminded me that he had met me three years before when I spoke at the Religious Emphasis Week there at the university. As he talked, I faintly remembered, and the more he talked the clearer the story came.

The young man had had neurological problems, which had caused long lapses of memory, stuttering speech, and inadequate motor control. He told me what it had meant to him for me to give him an hour of my time three years before, reminded me that he had written me afterward and shared some poetry and I had responded by mail.

Then came the shocker. "It was the love of my mother," he said, "and the attention and affirmation you gave that brought me to Christ and prevented me from destroying my life." Since then he had had three neurosurgeries and was on the road to wholeness. I came away from that young man, trembling inside.

Here was a person I didn't know—an encounter with whom it took some doing for me to recall—crediting me with a life-changing, life-saving experience. We never know the life and death difference what we do and the love we show might make in the life of another person. The possibility is open to all of us . . . the possibility of *an intercessory life.*

We are called to intercessory prayer; it is a part of our priesthood. But more, I believe the ultimate expression of our priesthood is to live an intercessory life.

> The call is not to *follow* Jesus, but to *abide* in Christ, to allow him free and full residence in our lives.

I believe the normal stance of a person who wants to be a faithful Christian is to be responsible *to* Christ, and have sought this responsibility throughout my ministry life. It has been only in the past few years, however, that I have become conscious of what I believe is a far greater responsibility—to be responsible *for* Christ. There is a difference.

To be responsible *to* Christ is to be accountable to him, to be and do what we think he would have us be and do. My hunch is that is the way most of us think about living our discipleship . . . being responsible *to* Christ.

We may have emphasized following Christ too much. This emphasis is too often distorted, reducing Christianity to the level of other religions and diminishing Jesus to merely an example for us to follow. This is one of Paul's greatest contributions to us; he kept calling us back from that pitfall, reminding us that the example of Jesus is only a part of the redeeming gospel. Were there no more than this, no more than Jesus as a great prophet and a great model, the contemplation of the perfect love and holiness of Jesus would only breed hopelessness.

The evangel of an ethical example is a devastating thing; it makes religion a grievous burden. The call is not to *follow* Jesus, but to *abide in* Christ, to allow him free and full residence in our lives. Indwelling us, he is not only the enabler of a new quality of life, he lives in us and we express his presence in the world.

Being responsible *for* Christ, then, is something different from following Christ, or being responsible *to* Christ. It is not seeking to be accountable to, or to please Christ; it is actually *being Christ in the world*, living and acting in our family and community as Christ living and acting there.

In one situation after another, Jesus identifies himself, in effect saying, "This is who I am."

- "I am the bread of life."
- "I am the resurrection and the life."
- "I am the Good Shepherd."
- "I am the door."
- "I am the vine."

One claim which illumines our thoughts about being responsible not *to* but *for* Christ is as familiar, maybe more than any of his other claims: "I am the light of the world. Whoever follows me will never walk in darkness but will have the light of life" (John 8:12).

Jesus not only said, "I am the light of the world," he said, "you are the light of the world." As radical as it may be, as Christ followers, we are what Jesus was and is . . . the light of the world.

Reflecting and Recording

Spend some time reflecting on your own life. Have you sought to live responsible *to* Christ, rather than *for* Christ?

During the Day

As you encounter persons and situations today, be deliberate in thinking whether you need to be responsive *to* Christ or *for* Christ.

DAY 23

You are the Light of the World

You are the light of the world. A city on a hill cannot be hidden. Neither do people light a lamp and put it under a bowl. Instead they put it on its stand, and it gives light to everyone in the house. In the same way, let your light shine before men, that they may see your good deeds and praise your Father in heaven.

—Matthew 5:14–16

If you'll recall from Days 15–21, it is not difficult to make the connection of this word of Jesus with his similar call to us: "Abide in me, and I will abide in you." As we abide in Christ, Paul's intercession for us is answered: "that Christ may dwell in your hearts in love . . . so may you attain to fullness of being, the fullness of God Himself" (Eph. 3:17, 19, NEB).

As we abide in Christ, we become responsible *for* Christ, living an intercessory life.

In 1982, I published a book entitled *Alive in Christ: The Dynamic Process of Spiritual Formation*. I defined spiritual formation as the "dynamic process of receiving through faith and appropriating through commitment, discipline, and action, the living Christ into our own life to the end that our life will conform to and manifest the reality of Christ's presence in the world." Long before writing that book, I had become convinced through a study of Paul and his New Testament writings that this is the core meaning of being Christian: to be alive in Christ, to live our lives "in Christ." As we grow in being alive in Christ, every part of our life is connected with Christ. We live in Christ (Col 2:6), and with Christ (Col. 2:13). We are instructed by Christ; his word dwells in us (Col. 3:16). To the degree of our yielding to the indwelling Christ, we manifest his presence in the world.

Through the past twenty-five years, I have come full circle but to a more radical understanding; essentially, a more powerful reality. To *manifest* is to *make apparent to the senses or the mind*, to *show plainly*, or *reveal*. Christ is dependent upon us not alone to "manifest," but to express his life in the world—and that is my definition of "an intercessory life."

This simple, but poignant story will point the direction in which we are to go. A seven-year-old boy from a poor family in New York was doing his bit to help the family survive. His mother set him up at the entrance of the New York subway with oranges and apples for sale. They had simply taken a tall fruit basket, turned it upside down, placed a board upon it and set four or five small baskets of apples and oranges on it. The hope was that weary workers on their way home by subway would purchase a piece of fruit to tide them over until dinner or a basket to take home to their family.

> As we abide in Christ, we become responsible for Christ, living an intercessory life.

The end-of-day rush started. Some hurrying person, running to catch the train, bumped into the makeshift stand and sent apples and oranges rolling in every direction. The crowd scurried on, with the exception of one man, who saw what happened—and saw the despair on the little boy's face as tears formed in the child's eyes—and set his briefcase down and began to collect the runaway fruit. He gathered as much as he could, put the fruit back in the baskets, replaced the baskets on the little stand, and hurried off to catch his train.

Overwhelmed by it all, the little boy shouted after him, "Hey Mister, are you Jesus?"

The story may be too simple and sentimental for sophisticated minds, but Jesus said, "A little child will lead them." How might we live that would evoke a response like that from someone to us?

Reflecting and Recording

1. Read the following definition of spiritual formation three or four times, reflecting on its meaning:

   Spiritual formation is the dynamic process of receiving through faith and appropriating through commitment, discipline, and action, the living Christ into our own life to the end that our life will conform to and manifest the reality of Christ's presence in the world.

❖ ❖ ❖

2. Now translate this definition into your own words, in the way you might share the definition with a friend.

During the Day

Look for a way to act in such a way that some person seeing you today will wonder as the little boy did: *Are you Jesus?*

DAY 24

Recovering the Meaning of Discipleship

*And he who searches our hearts knows the mind of the Spirit,
because the Spirit intercedes for the saints in accordance with God's will.*

—Romans 8:27

AN INTERCESSORY LIFE PROVIDES DIRECTION. WE HAVE PUT EMPHASIS ON intercessory prayer because that's a ministry to which we are called, but it also provides the dynamic for our living as Christ in the world. Hopefully the meaning of the way we expressed this in our first week of this venture is becoming clearer: Intercession is at the heart of our relationship to the Father, the risen and reigning Christ and to the Holy Spirit. Two verses of Scripture combine to give the picture.

Put Romans 8:27 with the exhilarating fact that Christ "always lives to intercede" for us, (Heb. 7:25) and you have the dynamic work of the Trinity: Father, Son, and Holy Spirit. God searches our minds; the Holy Spirit becomes the intercessor of our hearts; and as the Risen Lord, Jesus is the Great Intercessor, so the intercessions of the Holy Spirit and the Christ are one. As we abide in Christ, our intercession is one with the Holy Spirit and Christ, the Great Intercessor, in the throne room of heaven.

Our life as Christ-followers is guided by the same Spirit who guided Christ. In fact, The Holy Spirit is the divine power of Christ active in us. The more we cultivate that awareness and yield to that Presence, the more it is true: "it is not I who lives, but Christ lives in me" (Gal. 2:20).

As previously suggested, it is not enough to follow Jesus, trying to imitate him as much as possible. Jesus said, ". . . you are the light of the world." Our call is to be living Christs here and now, in our time and in our place.

With this in mind, Jesus' appearance after his resurrection and his commissioning the disciples provides clear direction for us:

> On the evening of that first day of the week, when the disciples were together, with the doors locked for fear of the Jewish leaders, Jesus came and stood among them and said, "Peace be with you!" After he said this, he showed them his hands and side. The disciples were overjoyed when they saw the Lord. Again Jesus said, "Peace be with you! As the Father has sent me, I am sending you." And with that he breathed on them and said, "Receive the Holy Spirit. If you forgive anyone's sins, their sins are forgiven; if you do not forgive them, they are not forgiven."—John 20:19–23

The grand narrative of God's nature is clear: God the Father sends the Son (John 3:17; 5:36; 6:57; Gal. 4:6; 1 John 4:9). The Father and the Son send the Holy Spirit (John 14:26; 15:26: Acts 2:23) and the Father Son and Holy Spirit send us, the church, into the world (Matt. 28:19–20; John 17:18; 20:21; Acts 1:8; 13:2–3). Jesus was the One sent. God, our Father, is the missionary God who sends; and we are sent ones.

Jesus always referred to himself as the sent one:

- "My food," he said, "is to do the will of him who sent me and to finish his work." (John 4:34)
- "He who receives you receives me, and he who receives me receives the one who sent me." (Matt. 10:40)

Our problem (in the Western world, particularly) is that as the Christian faith and way became the general way of culture and as we became a kind of "Christendom," the dominant vision of the Gospel made it possible to believe that salvation was something one could have apart from submitting one's whole life to the rule and reign of God. Discipleship, then, was separated from being a Christian; discipleship was optional. We could be Christian without being "called" to be a disciple, without being "sent."

> It is not enough to follow Jesus, trying to imitate him as much as possible.

This is not in harmony with the gospel's call to discipleship, and Jesus as the sent One Who, in turn, sends us. Discipleship, rightly understood, is the process or lifestyle by which we are able and continue to grow in knowing God, by receiving and responding to the good news of God's invitation to enter God's Kingdom mission in the world. That means that any version of the gospel that isn't a call to discipleship, that leaves discipleship as optional, is not the gospel Jesus preached: "As the Father has sent me, I am sending you."

DAY 24: RECOVERING THE MEANING OF DISCIPLESHIP

Reflecting and Recording

1. Spend a few minutes meditating on this word of Jesus: "He who receives you receives me, and he who receives me receives the one who sent me."

✤ ✤ ✤

2. What does this say about each one of us who are Christ followers being Christ's presence in the world?

✤ ✤ ✤

During the Day

The following verses are our memory passage for this week. Take it with your wherever you go during these next days. Take opportunity to reflect on it as you commit it to memory.

> Again Jesus said, "Peace be with you! As the Father has sent me, I am sending you." And with that he breathed on them and said, "Receive the Holy Spirit. If you forgive anyone's sins, their sins are forgiven; if you do not forgive them, they are not forgiven." (John 20:21–23)

DAY 25

We Are the Sent Ones

"My food," said Jesus, "is to do the will of him who sent me and to finish his work. Don't you have a saying, 'It's still four months until harvest'? I tell you, open your eyes and look at the fields! They are ripe for harvest."

—John 4:34–35

WHY DO WE EVEN QUESTION IT? FORTY TIMES IN JOHN'S GOSPEL ALONE he mentions the importance of having been sent by the Father. God had to have someone on earth to represent Him, so He sent Jesus. Jesus needs us to represent himself, just as he represented the Father, so he sends us. The language could not be clearer: "As the Father has sent me, I am sending you" (John 20:21).

Notice the implications of Jesus' words. If his work is to do the will of the Father, he is sending us to do that same work: *"He who receives you receives me, and he who receives me receives the one who sent me"* (Matt. 10:40).

If we are Christian, our relationship with one another should be a relationship of Christ with the other. It's not difficult to think of Jesus' claim that if a person receives him, that person receives the Father, the one who sent Jesus. But how radical is this? "He who receives you receives me?" Think about that . . . think about it and tremble! We are living Christs here and now. As Jesus represented the Father who sent him, we represent Jesus who sends us.

It is this understanding that has enabled me to accept and respond to a word of Paul to the Colossians with which I have grappled through the years: "Now I rejoice in what was suffered for you, and I fill up in my flesh what is still lacking in regard to Christs' afflictions, for the sake of his body, which is the church." (Col. 1:24) The *Amplified Bible* adds "on our part" in the text, making it even more explicit that we are making up for what may be lacking in Christ's afflictions: "And in my own person I am making up whatever is still lacking and remains to be completed on our part of Christ's afflictions, for the sake of His body, which is the church."

DAY 25: WE ARE THE SENT ONES

The theme of redemption is written throughout everything Paul wrote. He repeats that theme over and over again in Colossians, affirming that God's implementation of His idea of redemption is the love gift of His Son Jesus Christ on the cross. We can't get away from this central theme. Paul's brilliant mind and his passion to present a convincing argument for the core substance of the Christian faith led him to place his comment that we "make up what was missing in Christ's affliction," immediately preceding the hinge verse of this Colossian letter—verse 27: "To them God has chosen to make known among the Gentiles the glorious riches of this mystery, which is Christ in you, the hope of glory."

> If we are Christian, our relationship with one another should be a relationship of Christ with the other.

Paul's definition of a Christian was "a person in Christ." His most vivid description of his own life in Christ was written to the Galatians, his autobiography is two sentences: "I have been crucified with Christ and I no longer live, but Christ lives in me. The life I now live in the body, I live by faith in the Son of God, who loved me and gave himself for me" (Gal. 2:20).

As we have insisted, Christ lives in us by the Holy Spirit. "The clue to the whole Christian experience, the core of the Gospel is that Christ, by whom and through whom all things were created, who is before all things and in all things, in whom God was pleased for all His fullness to dwell, the firstborn over all creation, the image of the invisible God; this Christ who has primacy over all things, in whom all things hold together, who is the head of the church—this Christ, who will stand at the end of time and be the final judge and triumphant Lord, *lives in us by the Holy Spirit.*

"This is not a sideline thought of Paul, not a peripheral detour of truth. This is the heart of it: Christ the Lord of Creation may live in us. *His dwelling in us is the hope of glory.*"[23]

When we get this—that Christ lives in us—we can understand how we humans can "fill up in my flesh what is lacking in regard to Christ's afflictions."

Reflecting and Recording

Spend a few minutes reflecting on this assertion: As Jesus represented the Father who sent him, we present Jesus who sends us. Make some notes recording your response. What does it mean? Do you believe it? How might believing it impact the way you live?

During the Day

Continue living with the challenging word of our memory verse, being mindful of all that you have been considering today.

DAY 26

Jesus' Ministry Re-presented by Christians

*Again Jesus said, "Peace be with you! As the Father has sent me,
I am sending you."*

—John 20:21

As Jesus represented the Father who sent Him, we represent Jesus who sends us.

A sent one is a representative, one who represents the sender. Dutch Sheets rightly makes the point that we don't literally re-do what Christ did; there was a once and for all-ness about Jesus' life, teaching, death, resurrection, and ascension. But we do 're-present' Christ. Sheets states it this way:

"He is the balm in Gilead (see Jer. 8:22), but we apply this healing salve.
"He is the fountain of life (see Jer. 2:13; 17:13), but we are dispensers of His living water.
"His is the comforting shepherd's staff (see Ps. 23:4), but He allows us the privilege of extending it.
"Think about it. The great Healer 'healing' through us; the great High Priest 'priesting' though us; the great Lover 'loving' through us."[24]

In his letter to the Church in Philippi, Paul wrote one of the most beautiful descriptions of Jesus we have in Scripture. We considered this on Day 21:

Let the same mind be in you that was in Christ Jesus, who, though he was in the form of God, did not regard equality with God as something to be exploited but emptied himself, taking the form of a slave being born in human likeness. And being found in human form, he humbled himself and became obedient to the point of death—even death on a cross. Therefore God also highly exalted him and gave him the name that is above every name, so that at the name of Jesus every knee should bend, in heaven and on earth and under the earth, and every tongue should confess that Jesus Christ is Lord, to the glory of God the Father.—Philippians 2:5–11, NRSV

> A sent one is a representative, one who represents the sender.

Not only is this a vivid description of Jesus, it is a call to us. Jesus is a servant. In him is embodied the self-giving God to persons, and also, the self-giving person to other persons. Jesus is the Lord who is servant, and the servant who is Lord. As our Lord, he calls his followers to be servants in his style, to the self-abandonment to the love of God and the love of neighbor that so clearly characterizes him.

Jesus leaves little doubt that it is a servant style to which he calls us. "Anyone who want to be great among you must be your servant . . . just as the Son of Man came not to be served but to serve" (Matt. 20:26–28).

Not only does Jesus call us to this style, he gives us life through this style: "Anyone who finds his life will lose it; anyone who loses his life for my sake will find it" (Matt. 10:39).

Reflecting and Recording

We referred above to our 're-presenting' Christ, using the metaphors of a balm in Gilead, fountain of living water, and the shepherd's staff. Think about these images and make some notes about how you have re-presented or sought to re-present Christ in these ways to someone you know.

- Balm in Gilead (healing)
- Fountain of living water (refreshing, cleansing)
- Shepherd's Staff (guiding)

During the Day

Look for the opportunity to re-present Christ to someone today.

DAY 27

In the Name of Christ, You Are Forgiven

At dawn he appeared again in the temple courts, where all the people gathered around him, and he sat down to teach them. The teachers of the law and the Pharisees brought in a woman caught in adultery. They made her stand before the group and said to Jesus, "Teacher, this woman was caught in the act of adultery. In the Law Moses commanded us to stone such women. Now what do you say?" They were using this question as a trap, in order to have a basis for accusing him.

But Jesus bent down and started to write on the ground with his finger. When they kept on questioning him, he straightened up and said to them, "Let any one of you who is without sin be the first to throw a stone at her." Again he stooped down and wrote on the ground.

At this, those who heard began to go away one at a time, the older ones first, until only Jesus was left, with the woman still standing there. Jesus straightened up and asked her, "Woman, where are they? Has no one condemned you?"

"No one, sir," she said.

"Then neither do I condemn you," Jesus declared. "Go now and leave your life of sin."

—John 8:1–11

LET'S LOOK AT AN INTERCESSORY LIFE, A LIFE *IN CHRIST*, IN THE CONTEXT OF humankind's most common needs, begining at the most fundamental level.

Our Christian faith journey begins with our acceptance of the incredible fact of our being unconditionally accepted by God. Each one of us is loved by God as though we were the only person in the world to love. There is a place in God's heart that only I can fill; and one that only you can fill. Our value in God is unquestionably affirmed once and for all by the gift of Jesus Christ in death on our behalf. As intercessors, we keep this in mind as we relate to others.

Tom, a man in a congregation I once served, was married and the father of three children—and having been arrested for aggressive, overt homosexual behavior, was also under the care of a psychiatrist. Only his wife knew; then he confided in me.

> Each one of us is loved by God as though we were the only person in the world to love.

He was finding meaning in his marriage, and his homosexual tendencies were latent; but he remained full of shame and guilt, felt unworthy, was becoming impotent in interpersonal elations, and on the verge of becoming a recluse. I invited him to participate in a small men's group, promising, of course, to keep his confidence always.

The men began to care about him, to share their lives with him, and he began to blossom as a person. Finally, he got the courage to share his ongoing sexual struggle privately with another man in the group. I was surprised when he told me about it. The other man was a picture of masculinity, almost a perverted kind of maleness (chauvinistic, some would say), and the last person I would have thought would understand Tom's struggle. But he did understand. He accepted Tom, continued to love him, and redemption took place.

Tom emerged from his guilt and self-condemnation, accepted God's forgiveness and acceptance, and became a redemptive force in that congregation. His redemption came through the intercessory acceptance of another.

Now shift to the need for forgiveness. No dynamic was more vividly present in Jesus than forgiveness. His encounter with the "sinful woman" caught in adultery (John 8:1–11) vivifies this dynamic.

In the story, Jesus is in a no-win dilemma. Men brought this woman to Jesus, asking him to pass judgment. In the Jewish religion, the penalty for adultery was death by stoning. If Jesus elected to show mercy on the woman and free her, he would be clearly disobeying the Jewish law. If he condemns her, or does not intervene in preventing condemnation he will go against everything he had taught about forgiveness and compassion.

Those who brought her to Jesus must have been shocked speechless by Jesus' response: "Let him who is without sin cast the first stone" (v. 7). Jesus then bends over and writes in the sand. Was he allowing the people some relief from their engagement with him in order that they might deal with their own consciences? Or, did he write something that probed even more deeply and burned more searingly upon their calloused hearts? We don't know, but we know that when he rose from writing, no one was present to condemn the woman. Jesus announced to her his forgiveness and call to a new life: "Neither do I condemn . . . go now and leave your life of sin" (v. 11).

Now recall our own study of Jesus appearing to his disciples after his resurrection and saying to them, "As the Father has sent me, I am sending you," and then giving them the Holy Spirit. Then he added this word, which has been debated by Christians ever since: "If you forgive anyone his sins, they are forgiven; if you do not forgive them, they are not forgiven."

This debated and debatable word calls for a revisit to the notion of our being intercessory people because we are a sent people: "As the Father has sent me, I am sending you." Jesus work continues through the ages through his servants. We Christians do no understand our mission in the world unless we realize that "we are ambassadors of Christ" . . . those who re-present him. We are not only to carry on his work in the world, we are to reproduce his attitude towards God and the world.

> He was sent to be 'the Light of the world'; so are we. He was sent to 'seek and to save that which was lost; so are we. He was sent not to do His own will, but the will of the /father that sent Him'; so are we . . . He was sent to pity, to look upon the multitude with compassion, to carry to them the healing of His touch, and the sympathy of His heart; so must we. We are the representatives of Jesus Christ . . . He is to be incarnated again in the hearts, and manifest again in the lives of His servants.[25]

The case is clear: Jesus parallels his action in sending us to the action of God in sending him. He uses the most dramatic dynamic he could use to underscore that: "If you forgive anyone his sins, they are forgiven; if you do no forgive them, they are not forgiven." It is the blood of Jesus that cleanses the sinner and sets him free; in that sense Jesus is the only one who can forgive. But we who have been sent by him, "breathed on by the Holy Spirit," are to do the priestly work of Jesus by speaking in the power of Jesus' name: "In the name of Christ, your sins are forgiven."

It is in this case of sin and forgiveness that our function as priests is desperately needed. We intercede in prayer for people who have lost their way, speaking to God for the people, praying that they will come to an awareness of sin and repent. We also speak to the people for God by letting them know that in the name of Christ, they are forgiven. It is this priestly action that will release people from the burden of sin.

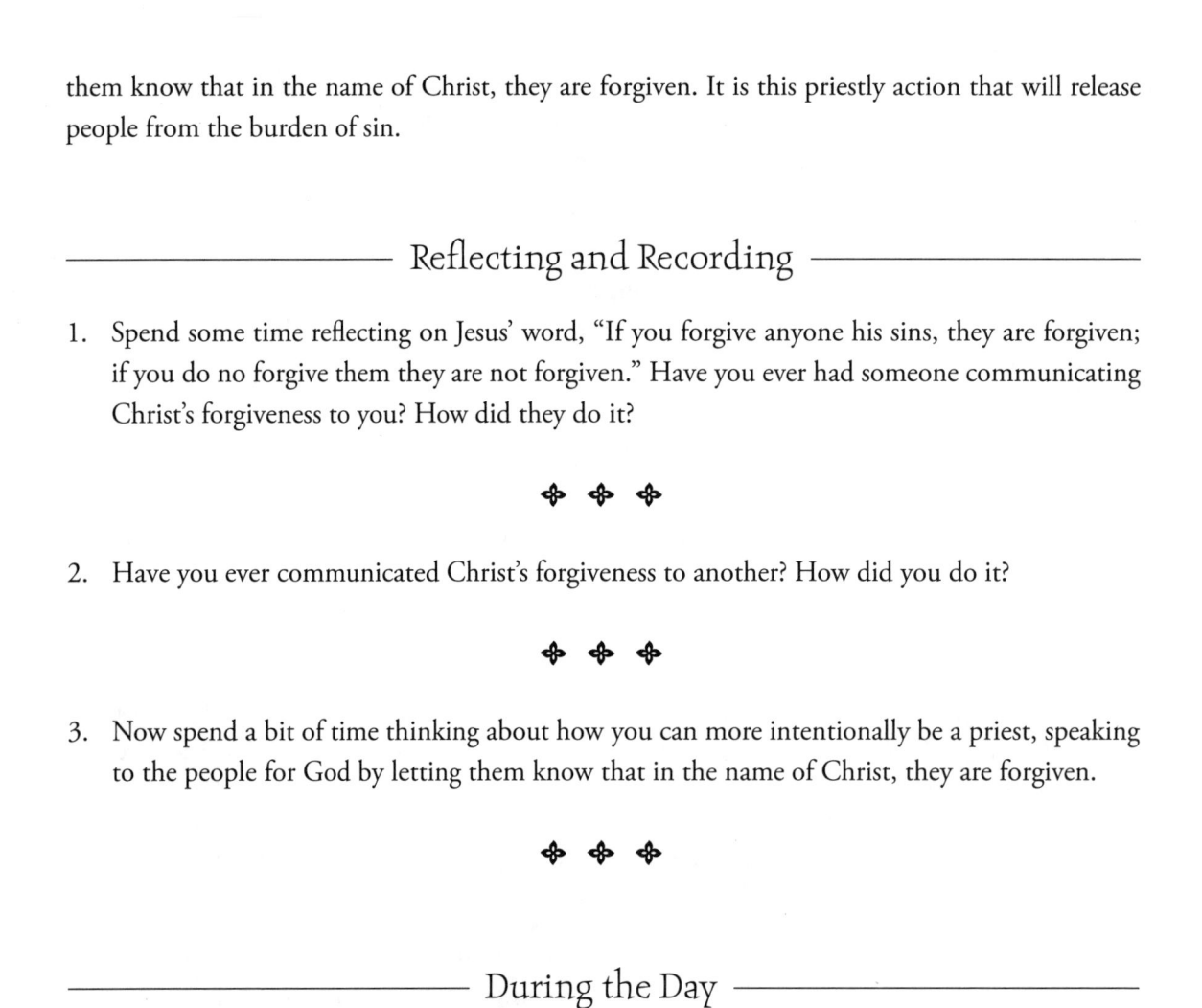

Reflecting and Recording

1. Spend some time reflecting on Jesus' word, "If you forgive anyone his sins, they are forgiven; if you do no forgive them they are not forgiven." Have you ever had someone communicating Christ's forgiveness to you? How did they do it?

✥ ✥ ✥

2. Have you ever communicated Christ's forgiveness to another? How did you do it?

✥ ✥ ✥

3. Now spend a bit of time thinking about how you can more intentionally be a priest, speaking to the people for God by letting them know that in the name of Christ, they are forgiven.

✥ ✥ ✥

During the Day

Be attentive to opportunities to be a priest for God . . . sensitive to the opportunity to intercede in prayer, to speak to God for a person who has shared a need; also, speaking to a person for God, assuring them of God's love, acceptance, and forgiveness.

DAY 28

Intercession is Meeting on Behalf of God

Therefore, if anyone is in Christ, he is a new creation; the old has gone, the new has come! All this is from God, who reconciled us to himself through Christ and gave us the ministry of reconciliation: that God was reconciling the world to himself in Christ, not counting men's sins against them. And he has committed to us the message of reconciliation.

—2 Corinthians 5:17–19

It is helpful here to consider again the Hebrew word for intercession: *paga,* meaning *to meet.* As we have already claimed, intercession is not alone a prayer we might pray; intercession is something we *do,* which can be done *through* prayer. Intercession (*paga*) is *meeting.* Praying and living in an intercessory fashion creates a meeting. When we pray and live an intercessory life, we meet with God and we meet with others. When we meet with others, we are meeting *as Christ* with others. This is our function as priests . . . meeting with God on behalf of people, meeting with people on behalf of God.

So, we can say to that person who is buried in self-pity and an overwhelming sense of worthlessness, with words and in the way we relate, you are accepted; you are a unique, unrepeatable miracle of God. There is a place in God's heart that only you can fill.

We can say to that person who has "missed the mark," and is full of shame and guilt, who thinks himself forever lost in the wilderness of sin, with words and in the way we relate, "in the name of Christ, you are forgiven."

Even in its secular meaning, *to intercede* means *to go between.* This is another dimension of *paga,* or meeting.[26] In our praying and in the style of an intercessory life, we meet . . . we go between for the sake of reconciliation. We act out our priesthood, and function as ambassadors . . . *as ones who have been sent.*

Through our *praying* and *relating*, we re-present and release what Christ did in his great act of reconciliation on the Cross. Some dear friends who have made a deliberate decision to live an intercessory life moved from a middle-class neighborhood to a near-slum area of our city. Before they moved into that neighborhood, they did prayer walks with other members of our congregation, met community residents, and requested that God save the families; protect the children; restore order and safety; and make the community a "place of good abode."

> We act out our priesthood, and function as ambassadors . . . as ones who have been sent.

Those prayer walks have been effective and our city knows that neighborhood has changed because of intercessory lives.

Our city, Memphis, is a very troubled city. A national magazine recently featured an article claiming Memphis as one of the least favorite cites in America in which to live. Poverty and the huge racial divide play a monumental role in our many troubles.

Our problems and our promise are currently focused on public education. We have had two public school districts in the metroplitan area: one, Memphis, primarily "the city," which was 85 percent black and poor; the other, Shelby County, "surburbia," which was 70 percent white and economically middle- and upper-middle class. In December 2011, the Memphis City School Board surrendered its charter, an action confirmed by a public referendum and a federal court order, forcing the creation of one school district to serve the city and the county.

The process repesented the largest school district consolidation in American history, and it came with major challenges of bridging chasms in race and class.

The Holy Spirit is leading some of us to believe that a huge part of the reconciliation/redemptive ministry to which Christ followers are called is public education. We have come to believe public education is the civil rights issue of the twenty-first century, and a person's zip code should not determine the quality of a child's educational opportunity. We Christians are called to re-present Jesus' care for "the least of these."

Our congregation acted boldly in an intercessory way. Three years ago, we established Cornerstone Prep, a private, explicitly Christian school, with very focused attention to providing education for the underserved children of our city. The school has had amazing results in providing education, proving that where a child lives does not determine learning potential. The educational measurements have exceeded national norms in every area, so our little school has gotten state and national attention.

In 2011, 950 of Tennessee's 1,750 public schools failed to make Adequate Yearly Progress (AYP). In the concentrated educational reform efforts of our state, eighty-five of these "failing" schools, sixty-nine of which are in Memphis, were targeted for intervention by the state. Through the Department of Education, our governor has established a district of these "failing" schools and has named a superintendent of that non-geographical district, charging him to reclaim those schools for effective education.

Lester School, the primary elementary school serving the Binghampton neighborhood, is among the sixty-nine failing schools in Memphis. In fact, Lester School is the lowest performing school in the entire state. When the opportunity arose for charter school groups to share in this "reclaiming" process for Lester School, the trustees of Cornerstone Prep made the deliberate decision to seek to bring more justice to the Binghampton Community. In order to accomplish this, Cornerstone Prep would have to give up being an explicitly Christian private school and become a charter school. This change in status would allow Cornerstone Prep to serve the larger public good in a manner currently not possible, enabling Cornerstone Prep to serve more than 800 Binghampton families. After a lengthy interview, application, and approval process, we have been given the responsibility for a failing school in the neighborhood where our church has for years focused its missional work. Jesus said, "unless a grain of wheat falls into the earth and dies, it remains just a single grain; but if it dies, it bears much fruit" (John 12:24). As those seeking to live an intercessory life, we believe that Cornerstone Prep must die as an explicitly Christian school, in order to serve a desperate and needy community. We are *not* giving up our Christian mission; rather, we are pursuing that mission in a different way. What we have been able to do in Christian witness and teaching in the classroom, we will now do after school, in accordance with the law. Our commitment to intercessory living will be tested.

> We are *not* giving up our Christian mission; rather, we are pursuing that mission in a different way.

Reflecting and Recording

1. Reflect on this claim: *through our praying and relating, we re-present and release what Christ did in his great act of reconciliation on the cross.* Do you think it may be so? How might it be so? Have you experienced anything like it in your praying and relating?

✣ ✣ ✣

2. What is the boldest self-giving action on behalf of others you have seen a group of people take.

✣ ✣ ✣

3. Do you see this action as intercession? In what way?

✣ ✣ ✣

During the Day

Your memory verse tells you that you are a sent one. Seek to let that fact shape your relationships today.

Group Meeting for Week Four

Introduction

Paul advised the Philippians, "Let your conversation be as it becometh the gospel of Christ" (Phil. 1:27, KJV). Our conversation—our speech—indicates the content of our life. Paul urged the Colossians, "Let your speech always be gracious, seasoned with salt," (Phil. 4:6) and admonished the Ephesians, "Let no evil talk come out of your mouths, but only what is useful for building up . . . so that your words may give grace to those who hear" (v. 29).

Most of us may not have experienced the dynamic potential of the conversation to which Paul calls the Philippians, but we need to be aware that life is found in communion with God and in conversation with others.

Speaking and listening with this sort of deep meaning is challenging. All of us have experiences that we cannot easily talk about. Genuinely listening to others and reflecting back what we have heard them say can help them think clearly and gain perspective. Listening, then, is an act of love. When we listen to someone, we say nonverbally: "I value you. You are important." When we listen in a way that makes a difference, we surrender ourselves to the other person, saying, "I will hear what you have to say and will receive you as I receive your words. When we speak in a way that makes a difference, we speak for the sake of others; thus we contribute to their understanding and wholeness.

Sharing Together

1. Ask someone ahead of time to open the meeting with prayer.
2. Ask if anyone would like to share something special that has happened this past week or two connected with using the book and sharing this forty-day journey.
3. Invite two or three people to read their rendering of the paragraph on Day 22 on being responsible *for* Christ. Then spend ten to fifteen minutes discussing what it means to be responsible *for* Christ rather than *to* Christ. Then discuss what it means for us to be "the light of the world" as Christ is "the light of the world."

4. Have someone read the definition of spiritual formation found in the Reflecting and Recording section of Day 23. Spend ten to fifteen minutes discussing this definition, especially noting the action words in the definition. What does it mean to 'receive through faith . . . the living Christ'? How do we appropriate through commitment, discipline and action, the living Christ into our lives? If the goal is to conform to and manifest the reality of Christ's presence in the world, then what does that mean about being Christ, and being responsible *for* Christ in the world?
5. Invite the group to turn to their Reflecting and Recording notes on Day 26. Spend some time asking persons to share their experiences of re-presenting Christ through being a "balm in Gilead" (healing), a "fountain of living water" (refreshing and cleansing), "shepherd's staff" (guiding).
6. Spend the balance of your time discussing discipleship. Is being a disciple an option for the Christian? If being a disciple means being "sent," who is sending and what is the purpose of our being sent?

Praying Together

Corporate prayer is one of the great blessings of the Christian community. We invite you to go deeper now, experimenting with the possibilities of prayer in a specific fashion.

1. Bow in silence and prayerful concern for the persons in your group. In your mind, picture each person—bringing to awareness what you know about that person as you have experienced him or her in your sharing together, and praying silently for each.
2. After this period of silence, the leader will name one by one each person in the group, inviting a volunteer to offer a verbal prayer after the person's name is called. The prayer may be brief—two or three sentences—or longer. The person offering the prayer will think of the person whose name is called. What concern or need has been shared tonight or in the past weeks that could be mentioned in prayer? You may want to express gratitude for the person's life and witness, the role he or she plays in the group, or that person's ministry in the community, possibly in a family situation. Someone may be seeking direction or confronting a crucial decision.

Continue until all group members have been prayed for. Close with a brief prayer for blessing and guidance for each person during the coming week.

WEEK FIVE
The Intercessor as Priest

DAY 29

The Priesthood of All Believers

But you are a chosen people, a royal priesthood, a holy nation, a people belonging to God, that you may declare the praises of him who called you out of darkness into his wonderful light. Once you were not a people, but now you are the people of God; once you had not received mercy, but now you have received mercy.

—1 Peter 2:9–10

IF YOU WERE ASKED TO NAME THE MOST SIGNIFICANT DOCTRINES OF PROTEStant Christianity, the two that would come to your mind immediately and would probably be named most frequently are: Justification by Grace through Faith, and the Priesthood of All Believers. I doubt if there has been a time since Martin Luther started that conflagration of religious revival and reformation when these two giant thoughts of Protestant Christianity have not been prominent in our thoughts. The ideas may come quickly to mind, but what do they mean?

Though Roman Catholic and Orthodox folks are very comfortable with it, the word "priest" has a sort of strangeness about it for most Protestants. Some Protestants even feel a bit uncomfortable using it. There has been a mystery surrounding the word that almost scares us. We are more comfortable talking about justification than about priesthood. Yet, it is at the heart of the Christian faith.

Not only so, the notion of "a priest to represent us" is residual in human nature, and all religions have something similar to it. F.B. Meyer expressed it this way:

> Every race, therefore, conscious on the one hand of God's majesty and holiness, and on the other, of its own unworthiness, has selected one of its number to stand as mediator between Him and themselves, hearing his voice, and uttering for them things which they dared not say. The consciousness of the gulf between the purity of the highest heavens and the impurity in which men have been shapen has acted as an impelling force, that could devise no better expedient than to seek representation by the fittest of their race."[27]

Priests are members of the community set apart to offer sacrifice and mediate between God and human beings. In the Old Testament there were three expressions of this priesthood: in a ritualistic kind of way with the Levitical priesthood (Ex. 28:1; 32:25–29; Lv. 8:1–9:24), as priest-king like Melchizedek (Gen. 14:18–20), and in a prophetic way, like Ezekiel. The writer of the Epistle to the Hebrews called Jesus the "great high priest"(Heb. 4:14–5:10), made so by God.

> Priests are members of the community set apart to offer sacrifice and mediate between God and human beings.

And Paul expressed it this way in his first Letter to Timothy: "For there is one God and one mediator between God and mankind, the man Christ Jesus" (1 Tim. 2:5).

At the time of the Reformation, the priesthood had become so rigidly formalized that only the priest could have direct access and offer sacrifice to God. Other believers had to have an intermediary (a priest) to receive forgiveness. The Reformation principle of the Priesthood of all Believers declared that all believing Christians had the privilege and freedom to stand before God in personal communion through Christ, confessing and receiving forgiveness without another human intermediary. But there is far more in that principle.

Though there is an "ordained" priesthood/ministry in Protestant Christianity, with ordination having different meaning in different expressions of the church, the common conviction is that all believers share in Christ's royal priesthood (1 Peter 2:9), which is called the "priesthood of all believers" or "of all the faithful."

Peter used the language of "priest" to give us a good picture of our identity and function as God's people. In fact, that's what Peter calls Christians, "God's own people":

DAY 29: THE PRIESTHOOD OF ALL BELIEVERS

As you come to (Christ), the living Stone—rejected by humans but chosen by God and precious to him you also, like living stones, are being built into a spiritual house to be a holy priesthood, offering spiritual sacrifices acceptable to God through Jesus Christ. For in Scripture it says:

"See, I lay a stone in Zion, a chosen and precious cornerstone, and the one who trusts in him will never be put to shame." Now to you who believe, this stone is precious. But to those who do not believe,

"The stone the builders rejected has become the cornerstone," and, "A stone that causes people to stumble and a rock that makes them fall." . . . But you are a chosen people, a royal priesthood, a holy nation, God's special possession, that you may declare the praises of him who called you out of darkness into his wonderful light. Once you were not a people, but now you are the people of God; once you had not received mercy, but now you have received mercy.—1 Peter 2:1–7, 9–10

It follows then that as persons "in Christ," our being priests is in the pattern of our High Priest, Jesus, who "ever lives to make intercession." We are to live an intercessory life.

Reflecting and Recording

1. If you were asked, "Tell me what a priest is," what would you say in two or three sentences? Why?

✤ ✤ ✤

2. Spend a few minutes thinking of how you live the Christian faith. How does your way of living harmonize with the fact that as a Christian you are a priest?

✤ ✤ ✤

During the Day

Verses 9–10 of the passage above will be our new memory passage. Copy it and carry it with you during the coming days. Read it often to commit it to memory. As you do, reflect on what it means to be a part of a royal priesthood.

DAY 30

Exercising Our Calling as Priests

Therefore, holy brothers, who share in the heavenly calling, fix your thoughts on Jesus, the apostle and high priest whom we confess. He was faithful to the one who appointed him, just as Moses was faithful in all God's house. . . . But Christ is faithful as a son over God's house. And we are his house, if we hold on to our courage and the hope of which we boast.

—Hebrews 3:1–2, 6

STACEY FERGUSON BEGAN THE FIRST GRADE IN SEPTEMBER, 1973, AS THE DAUGHTER of one of the organizers of the Citizens Against Bussing. At the time, she wasn't old enough to understand, but in retrospect, she said, "I witnessed how fear without faith could destroy an educational system."

At a summer camp in 1979, Stacey met a person who became her best friend that week: "She was better than me in most ways, especially academically, and she was African American." This made her question why her family had lived under financial stress to send her to a private school. A question and a seed were planted in her heart.

Fast forward to December 2010. On Day 28, I told of a part of our church's response to the education crisis in Memphis. The Memphis City School Board surrendered its charter, which legally required the establishment of a new school district, integrating the city and the county systems. It was this event that galvanized Stacey's commitment to prayer and her leadership in organizing a county/city-wide prayer meeting. This was her witness:

> The Lord had convicted me of a need to pray, daily, a year earlier. I was meeting with Him in the mornings with Bible in hand at 5:30, before my family awoke. He brought me there, so I would know His voice and would be in a discipline ready to answer His call. This is where the praying began. On my knees, I met with the God of the universe to pray for healing for our school system.

DAY 30: EXERCISING OUR CALLING AS PRIESTS

I prayed for each article and each name mentioned in the newspaper. I prayed for wisdom and a banishment of all things (fear, anxiety, ignorance) that had the potential of tearing the community apart like the 1971–1973 bussing movement did. I could see the Lord's hand in every bit of it. The tearing down of broken walls that kept us from being all that we could be. I could see him lifting people up and causing archenemies to make peaceful agreements.

Hundreds of people in our county and city are praying daily for this demanding process which is so complex and complicated, believing that God wants the very best for his children and that education is a part of that "best." Stacey is leading us in that effort in a "Pray for Our Schools" movement. She sends us a weekly prayer focus. We gather at least monthly, and there are praying persons at every meeting of the school board and design team for the emerging school district. Our hearts and spirits prayerfully brood, silently groaning in intercession for God to birth a school system that is not only excellent in its educational mission, but is redemptive and reconciling for our wounded and desperately needy city.

> Faith sees the invisible, believes the unbelievable, and receives the impossible.
> —Corrie Ten Boom

We pray for the teachers and administrative staff; the state legislature and court process; the school board and the transition planning commission; and especially for the children. In a recent prayer letter, Stacey called us to "pray for the protection from all that the children are seeing and hearing from the adults in this process. May their hearts be guarded from anything that is not edifying or holy in God's sight. May prejudice and disrespect be bound from their hearts and minds. May they see God's people acting in accordance with the faith that they profess so freely on Sunday."

In leading this prayer effort, Stacey reminds us of a word from Corrie Ten Boom: "Faith sees the invisible, believes the unbelievable, and receives the impossible."

The eyes of the nation are on Memphis because of our racial issues and economic problems, and our "broken" public education system—but also because of our efforts and bold experiments in education reform. Some of us believe that God is going to do something spectacular in this arena of education, proving that if it can happen in Memphis, it can happen anywhere in the nation. We also believe that this event will bear witness to God's faithful response to trusting people who prayed while believing. In the meantime, not only do we continue to pray, we seek to live intercessory lives by exercising our calling as priests.

Reflecting and Recording

1. Looking back over your Christian life, what is the most meaningful prayer group or movement you have been a part of? Make some notes describing that experience . . . what was going on in your life? How did you become involved? Were there particular issues/circumstances that brought the group together?

❖ ❖ ❖

2. Is there an issue in your community presently that is getting the prayer energy of an organized prayer effort? Are you a part of it? If there is an issue that calls for an organized effort, might God be calling you to get involved?

❖ ❖ ❖

During the Day

Talk with at least one person today about a particular need for prayer in your own life and/or in the community. If you feel there needs to be an organized effort, discuss that with the person.

DAY 31

Our Identity and Purpose

I will plant her for myself in the land; I will show my love to the one I called 'Not my loved one.' I will say to those called 'Not my people,' 'You are my people'; and they will say, 'You are my God.'

—Hosea 2:23

Peter begins his identification of Christ followers by quoting the Old Testament prophet, Hosea, almost verbatim. And since Peter is so rooted in Old Testament scripture, he begins to apply title after title after title upon these individuals who have been loved into redemptive being by God Himself. Peter calls them a chosen people, a royal priesthood, a holy nation, God's own people.

That's who we are—a chosen people, chosen by God. We have been called into redemptive being by God Himself.

Peter is so excited about what he has to say and what he wants to put down on paper that he almost stumbles over himself, lest he misses any detail: "You are a chosen people, a royal priesthood, a holy nation, a people belonging to God, that you may declare the praises of him who called you out of darkness into his wonderful light" (1 Peter 2:9). Our identity and purpose is summed in that one sentence.

- Our identity: God's own people.
- Our function: to declare the wonderful deeds.

As God's own people, we are witnesses, representatives, priests. To reiterate, as priests, we speak to God for the people. This is our ministry of prayer, especially intercession. We also speak to the people for God. This is our ministry of witnessing, being God's agent, sharing our story in word, deed, and sign. The intercessory life is a pattern of God's action in our life and the life of the world.

Bill Martin was a member of a congregation I served. He was a recovering alcoholic who worked zealously at his Christian faith and his recovery. He had a quaint way of expressing himself; in fact, I think he deliberately worked on how he would say things in order to guarantee attention. In a note to me, following a sermon I had preached on the priesthood of all believers, he wrote, "I want you to know I got it: *an agent of God I am.*" Well, he had gotten it. That's what it means to be a priest. We are *agents of God*. We speak to the people for God, and we speak to God for the people.

This suggests a dimension of intercession that too many miss. There is a kinship between prophetic action and prophetic declaration. We could have talked about this when we discussed intercession as prayer, but it seems more appropriate here when we think of acting and speaking as agents (priests) of God. We may speak in a *foretelling* (predicting) or *forthtelling* (actions or words) way. In either case, we proclaim God's will as we have been led by the Holy Spirit in perceiving. When we are directed by God to speak, we must do so and likewise, when we are called to act. We may not completely understand either, but we must obey.

> As priests, we speak to God for the people. We also speak to the people for God.

Dutch Sheets reminds us that "prophetic words or actions prepare a way, in the same sense that John the Baptist, the prophet, prepared the way with his words and actions for the Messiah to come and for the glory of the Lord to be revealed (see Isa. 40:1–5). Prophetic ministry (the intercessory life) releases the way for the glory of the Lord and the ministry of Jesus to follow. Prophetic actions and declarations prepare the way for God to work on earth."[28]

John Woolman was a person whose prophetic actions and declarations eventually contributed to the freeing of slaves in the United States. He was a Quaker, described as a quiet man "whose faithfulness spoke loudly in tempestuous times." At twenty-one, he left the family farm and was apprenticed to a shop owner where he learned the trade of a tailor. He also became qualified to draft legal documents. Even at this early age, he was soon confronted with the institution of slavery when his employer instructed him to write a bill of sale for his slave. He struggled in his soul and shared with his employer that he "believed slavekeeping to be a practice inconsistent with the Christian religion."

DAY 31: OUR IDENTITY AND PURPOSE

He became successful, soon taking over his employer's dry-goods business, adding an orchard business of his own, and becoming moderately prosperous. He soon became concerned that his business was taking an inordinate amount of his time and energy and he deliberately pared down his business enterprise and gave time to an itinerate ministry of priestly/prophetic teaching. On a ministry trip to the South, he saw slavery firsthand and desribed it as "a dark gloominesss hanging over the Land."

Later, when a Quaker friend, fearful that he might not live because of a bad accident, sent for John to write his will, John wrote it, refusing to put anything in the will that would give a young Negro woman slave to one of the man's children. They had a discussion about it, and at length, the man agreed to set her free, and John finished his will.

Though John Woolman spoke powerfully, his actions were even more powerful. On one occasion, he had preached with bold convictions against slavery at a Quaker meeting and was taken to the home of Tomas Woodward for dinner. When he arrived, he saw servants all about and enquired of their status. When he was told they were slaves, he quietly left the home without a word. The silent testimony was so powerful that the next morning Tomas Woodward freed all of his slaves, despite the vigorous objections of his wife.

--- Reflecting and Recording ---

1. Spend a few minutes reflecting on the terms Peter applied to the Christian Community:

   - Chosen race
   - Royal priesthood
   - Holy nation
   - God's own people

❖ ❖ ❖

2. Does the faith community of which you are a part claim to be any of these? How is that awareness expressed?

3. How do you see yourself as "an agent of God"?

❖ ❖ ❖

———————————— During the Day ————————————

Continue your memory work. As you register the fact that you are a part of a royal priesthood, remember a priest speaks to God for the people and to the people for God. Seek to perform those functions more than once today.

DAY 32

Over-bearing or Under-bearing

Dear brothers and sisters, if another Christian is overcome by some sin, you who are godly should gently and humbly help that person back onto the right path. And be careful not to fall into the same temptation yourself. Share each other's troubles and problems, and in this way obey the law of Christ. If you think you are too important to help someone in need, you are only fooling yourself. You are really a nobody. Be sure to do what you should, for then you will enjoy the personal satisfaction of having done your work well, and you won't need to compare yourself to anyone else. For we are each responsible for our own conduct.

—Galatians 6:1–5, NLT

Yesterday, we discussed the prophetic action of John Woolman. He refused to include the "gifting of a slave" in a will he was asked to write. He also quietly, but dramatically, left a home in which he was visiting because there were so many slaves there. But as agents of God, our roles are not confined to major events or acquaintances—our roles also extend to our everyday lives, which include personal relationships.

In his Letter to the Galatians, Paul underscored the life of a Christ follower quite clearly; we are to carry each other's burdens, and by doing so, we fulfill the law of Christ. He said the same thing to the Corinthians: "If any member suffers, all suffer together. If one member is honored, all rejoice together."

He said it again to the Romans: "It is the duty of those who are strong to bear the weaknesses of those who are not strong."

How have we missed it? We are ministers, one to another. It is laced throughout the New Testament, and especially throughout Paul's writings. The term *laos,* from which we derive *laity* or *layman,* means the whole people of God. Therefore, a universal ministry should spring forth from within the church.

Two verses in the sixth chapter of this Letter to the Galatians express a tension that teaches us about this priesting ministry. In verse 5, Paul says, "Every man must shoulder his own pack." More traditional translations read, "Every man must bear his own burden." Yet in verse 2, Paul has already said, "Carry one another's burdens and so live out the law of Christ." So, which is it?

Two truths are revealed in the tension. One, no one can solve someone else's problems for him. I'm talking about personal problems that have to do with our emotions, our wills, our decision-making—not about the problems of living that require the expertise of a mechanic, or a dentist, or a lawyer, or a plumber. I'm talking about the problems that are rooted in the self and our potential—who we are as persons.

If we are going to take seriously our call as Christians to be priests to one another, we need to realize that we can share with a person, listen to him, respond to him, but we can't solve his problems. As I think of the ministry of Jesus, I can't remember his handing out easy solutions or offering pat answers to people's agonizing questions. He did enable people to find answers but those answers were, more often than not, within the persons themselves or within the possibility of a relationship. It was as though Jesus was always asking two questions: *What do you want most in life, and what are you willing to do to get it?* It may be that the only ministry we can perform with some people is to help them ask themselves those questions and to share with them as they clarify their answers.

> As agents of God, our roles are not confined to major events or acquaintances— our roles also extend to our everyday lives.

This is important in our relationships and in our efforts to minister to others. Many of us fall into a pattern that may be labeled "over-bearing,"—that is, seeking to bear too much of the burdens of others. We think we have to give advice or provide answers. We are unable to accept the fact that some people, given the freedom God has given us, are going to choose death over life. Though shocking, that's just the way it is, and the more we try to impose life upon them, the more determined they become in their pursuit of death. The classic example of this is the relation of a person to an alcoholic spouse. In my experience with innumerable alcoholics, I've never known one to choose the way of sobriety until his spouse released him and ceased struggling to solve his problem for him. We need to keep this perspective. We can't solve other people's problems for them.

DAY 32: OVER-BEARING OR UNDER-BEARING

Now, the second truth that emerges seems contradictory: No one can solve his own problems himself. How can that be? If no one can solve someone else's problems, how can say no one can solve his own problems by himself?

We look for balance. We are made for community, for relationship. We are not whole persons in isolation from other human beings. We may think we are sufficient unto ourselves, that we need only our own resources. But the ball eventually bounces down at one point: a built-in interdependency in life that none of us can escape.

> A Christian style of caring is a wholesome interdependence, a recognition that we belong to each other.

Though it is easy to fall into a pattern of over-bearing, I caution you about the opposite extreme—that of under-bearing. While some of us seek to bear too much of the burden of others, others fall into the under-bearing snare, that is, caring and bearing too little. A Christian style of caring is neither a smothering dependence or an indifferent independence, but a wholesome interdependence, a recognition that we belong to each other. In the tension of these two verses there is the suggestion of *mutual ministry* which defines the dynamic of the *priesthood* of all believers.

We are ministers, and we are ministered to. This is what the priesthood of believers is all about.

Reflecting and Recording

1. In your journal, briefly describe an experience of trying to solve someone else's problems and how that effort came out.

❖ ❖ ❖

2. Look at your nuclear family, or a small group with whom you send time. Who among them try to solve other peoples' problems? Who are too expectant of help from others? Who is guilty of over-bearing or under-bearing? How do you relate to them as a priest?

❖ ❖ ❖

―――――― During the Day ――――――

Remember these persons throughout the day, offering brief prayers for them. This is practicing your priesthood . . . speaking to God for the people. If possible, engage at least one of these persons in a discussion about over-bearing and under-bearing. This may give you an opportunity to speak to a person for God.

DAY 33

The Priest as a Pattern of an Intercessory Life

Your brother, Aaron, and his sons, Nadab, Abihu, Eleazar, and Ithamar, will be set apart from the common people. They will be my priests and will minister to me. Make special clothing for Aaron to show his separation to God—beautiful garments that will lend dignity to his work. Instruct all those who have special skills as tailors to make the garments that will set Aaron apart from everyone else, so he may serve me as a priest. They are to make a chestpiece, an ephod, a robe, an embroidered tunic, a turban, and a sash. They will also make special garments for Aaron's sons to wear when they serve as priests before me. These items must be made of fine linen cloth and embroidered with gold thread and blue, purple, and scarlet yarn.

—Exodus 28:1–5, NLT

IN THE PAST FEW DAYS, WE HAVE CONSIDERED THE PRIESTHOOD OF ALL BELIEVers. The function of the priest is the pattern for an intercessory life. This is confirmed by the priesthood in Israel's early history serving as an image of intercession. Let's take a closer look at that priesthood.

The Tabernacle, the first formal meeting place of God and God's people, is described in Exodus 36–38; the garments of Aaron, the priest, are also described in Exodus 39. Every part of the elaborately prescribed dress of the high priest was significant, two of them particularly significant as we think about the nature of the priesthood of all believers and intercession.

The *ephod* was a kind of waistcoat in two pieces connected at the shoulders, one covering the chest and the other covering the back. On each of the shoulder pieces that connected the front and the back was a socket of gold, each pocket holding a sardonyx stone The names of the twelve tribes of Israel were carved on these stones in the order of their seniority.

The presence of these stones on the High Priest's shoulders proclaimed an important truth for the people. The priest entered the sanctuary as a representative of the entire nation; the interests, concerns, sins, and sorrows of the people were on his shoulders.

> The concerns of our community should be borne on our shoulders as we travail in intercession before the Lord.

The *breastplate* of the High Priest was composed of folded cloth in which there were twelve precious stones, lodged in four rows of three, with each stone containing the name of one of the tribes. So when the priest entered the Holy of Holies, he bore on his shoulders and over his heart the twelve tribes. His very presence at the place of worship was an act of intercession for the people. This was a responsibility for the High Priest, and a blessing for the people. These people were on his heart. None were excluded, from Dan to Beersheba, from the Jordan to the Mediterranean.

One can imagine that for several weeks before the great Day of Atonement, people would stand in line at the tent of the High Priest all day long—some maybe coming under the shadow of night—to share personal sorrows, temptations, illness, or confessions, saying or perhaps pleading, 'Remember me when you stand before the altar on the Holy Day. I will be outside, offering my heart, but you will be in the Holy of Holies, please don't forget me.'

> How much they needed a compassionate nature, that could be touched with the feeling of their infirmities and sorrows, and one who would be faithful, not dissipating on himself, or upon lesser concerns, those holy moments when he was face to face with God. In order to secure some certainty that they would be remembered they set their names on his person, so that the very stones would speak for them. "Aaron shall bear the names of the children of Israel in the breastplate of judgment upon his heart . . . for a memorial before the Lord continually" (Ex. 28:29).[29]

While we recognize that Aaron and the Levitical priesthood as one area of development in the worship life of Israel and the priesthood system itself was limited to that period of Israel's life with God, there is great meaning for us in the symbol of the names of the twelve tribes carried on the High Priest's shoulders and heart. Our circle of acquaintances should be carried in our heart—and always taken before the Lord in our prayers. The concerns of our community should be borne on our shoulders as we travail in intercession before the Lord.

DAY 33: THE PRIEST AS A PATTERN OF AN INTERCESSORY LIFE

The notion of *representation* on the part of the priest is the connection with the priesthood of all believers and intercession. As Christians, we have the privilege and freedom to stand before God in personal communion through Christ, confessing and receiving forgiveness without another human intermediary.

Though there is an 'ordained' priesthood/ministry, all Christians share in Christ's royal priesthood: "As you come to him, the living Stone—rejected by humans but chosen by God and precious to him—you also, like living stones, are being built into a spiritual house to be a holy priesthood, offering spiritual sacrifices acceptable to God through Jesus Christ" (1 Peter 2:4–5).

Or, in the words of my friend Bill Martin, "an agent of God I am."

Reflecting and Recording

1. Think of two or three people for whom you have been praying. In what sense or in what way have you been representing them to God in your praying?

❖ ❖ ❖

2. As you think about these persons, is there something you need to do or say, some way of relating to them that would re-present Christ to them?

❖ ❖ ❖

During the Day

Imagine yourself in some way carrying the persons you have been praying for *on* you or *with* you through the day. You are their priest and the Holy of Holies can be any where and any time you choose to go deliberately into God's presence. Seek to represent these persons to God in prayer and to represent God to them in word and action.

DAY 34

Responding as Priests to Two Common Needs

Father, I want those you have given me to be with me where I am,
and to see my glory, the glory you have given me because you loved me before
the creation of the world.

Righteous Father, though the world does not know you, I know you,
and they know that you have sent me. I have made you known to them,
and will continue to make you known in order that the love you have for me
may be in them and that I myself may be in them.

—John 17:24–26

Remember that Christ indwells us and the Holy Spirit empowers us; Jesus underscored this in the above prayer, yet feelings of inadequacy can be a major roadblock to our work of intercession. With Christ indwelling us, however, our adequacy or inadequacy must never be the issue.

We can overcome this feeling with an awareness of two basic human needs *to have others who will listen non-judgmentally* and *to help people understand and accept their feelings.*

The first one is difficult to practice because we are taught to test feelings, to challenge positions, to offer advice, but what people really *need* is none of that. They need us to listen non-judgmentally—and each of us is capable of this type of ministry. We can listen to people and by doing so, letting them know that "you are not alone, I hear you." When we start a relationship in that fashion, it is as though we are tenderly moving our spiritual fingers about the life of another person, feeling the pain and listening to the tones of that person until there is the kind of opening that enables us to share who we are and where we've been, what we know, and what we have experienced in a way that ministers precisely to the needs of that person. It also provides us the information we need about the person for more effective intercession. In fact, this kind of listening *is* intercession.

The problem is that most of us want to give answers to questions people are not asking. What we really need to do is to put ourselves in a responsive mode where we can focus on the other person and let the other person have her time in sharing what is going on in her life. We can do that.

The second basic human need to be aware of is *helping people understand and accept their feelings.* We all have feelings we don't understand—some of which we may be ashamed. Feelings we can't accept as real; though they are raging within: the near-hate or the actual hate we feel when our spouse spurns our love; the jealousy that comes on unexpectedly; the desire to hoard, to hold on to rather than to share; the morbid fear of death or the future. Sometimes our feelings are so ugly and distasteful to us, so deep and mysterious, so counter to our self-perceptions that we are fearful of them, so much so that we are unwilling to trust another with them. We are afraid if our feelings are unacceptable to us, they will certainly be unacceptable to others. We fear that persons will not accept our feelings, and by not accepting our feelings, they will reject us.

This is an opportunity for intercession . . . to communicate concern to another to the point that the other will trust her feelings to us. Accepting another's feelings non-judgmentally is a way of speaking for God. When we receive those feelings as a positive gift from the person, we affirm and enable her to face, process, and understand so that growth may ensue. This is the way change takes place.

> Most of us want to give answers to questions people are not asking.

I had almost forgotten about Ben when his letter arrived from Mississippi. I was in California, but the miles diminished as I read his penciled words on lined paper from a 25-cent tablet. The grammar wasn't correct, but I knew what Ben was saying.

He had seen my name in the county's weekly newspaper. I had been to my hometown, Richton, Mississippi, to visit my mother and father and the newspaper recorded that event, along with the account of church suppers, school programs, lodge meetings, hospital patients, and funerals. A bit provincial for a reader of the *Los Angeles Times*, but life and death for Ben. He read my name and had the grace to write me a note, just to see how I was doing.

His letter is a treasure, because I remembered Ben. I had been his pastor for five years. He was a so-called 'red-neck'; I was a so-called 'liberal.' But we were friends. I had often listened to Ben's raging tirades against blacks (He used a more offensive word).

Ben knew I listened to him, and I knew Ben listened to me. More than that, Ben's letter tells me that he knew I heard those fears, doubts, and longings that were behind his words—feelings of inadequacy, emptiness, frustration, and despair.

I was with Ben when his wife, Nona, died. Ironically, Ben disagreed with much of my preaching, but he invited me to preach Nona's funeral; I did, and then spent hours with Ben in the lonely aftermath. Later, he didn't quite have the conviction and courage to stand up for me when the church officials became angry at my witness in regards to race relations and reconciliation, but that's okay—I have Ben's letter and the space between the lines and the efforts behind the words are enough. Ben thanked me for listening to him, understanding his feelings, and being his friend. He wished he could have seen me while I was in Richton.

> We can function at these two levels of desperate need: one, non-judgmental listening, and two, helping others to understand, accept and maybe change their feelings.

There was a P.S. to his letter that climaxed my joy: "I think you could make it now as a preacher in Mississippi."

It was my turn. I wrote Ben a letter. I told him a lot of things about how I had valued our relationship, and how I missed the unique expression of Mississippi hospitality. I challenged him to continue to grow in his acceptance of people culturally and racially different from him, and to find relationships where that growth could take place. It all added up to this, "Ben, I love you and God loves you."

No matter what our gifts, we can function at these two levels of desperate need: one, non-judgmental listening, and two, helping others to understand, accept and maybe change their feelings. Knowing this, we can overcome our feelings of inadequacy which is the primary road block to our being priests to one another.

Reflecting and Recording

1. Recall an occasion when someone listened to you non-judgmentally. What did you share and how did they respond?

DAY 34: RESPONDING AS PRIESTS TO TWO COMMON NEEDS

❖ ❖ ❖

2. Can you recall an experience when your sharing (speaking and listening) with another freed them to share their feelings and enabled them to accept themselves and their feelings? Make some notes abut this experience.

❖ ❖ ❖

3. Do you see the work of a priest and intercession in these two instances of listening and sharing?

——————————— During the Day ———————————

Continue living with and repeating your memory verse.

DAY 35

Intercession as a Wrestling Match

Finally, be strong in the Lord and in his mighty power. Put on the full armor of God so that you can take your stand against the devil's schemes. For our struggle is not against flesh and blood, but against the rulers, against the authorities, against the powers of this dark world and against the spiritual forces of evil in the heavenly realms.

—EPHESIANS 6:10–12

THERE IS A SENSE IN WHICH INTERCESSION AS A FORM OF PRAYER MAY BE BEST described with the word *wrestle*. This is important to remember as we consider our lives as priests. In our speaking to God for the people, we sometimes have to wrestle. Ellsworth Kalas expresses it in a challenging way when he talks about his work as a pastor:

> When I enter a sick room, where a malignancy is about its hellish business, I cannot reach in with my hand and extract it. But I can wrestle with hell by my prayers, and I do. When I read in the papers of corruption in high places, I cannot always throw my intellectual commitments into the battle, especially when that corruption is in parts of the world where I have no vote—but I can wrestle in prayer. When some human being comes to my study with a burden too heavy to bear, there are instances where no advice matters and no change of facts can be affected. But I can push hell back for a time. I can stand beside God and claim His will for an oppressed human soul. This is prayer as wrestling. It is our ultimate weapon in our struggle with all that is wrong with our universe.[30]

David Brainerd was a great missionary to India. He came out of one of his great wrestling periods in prayer, saying, "My joints were loosed; the sweat ran down my face and body as if it would dissolve." That confession of Brainerd calls to mind Jesus wrestling in Gethsemane.

But wrestling is not limited to just our prayer lives. If we're seeking to achieve integrity that cannot be bought or sold, if we're seeking a courage that will not bend in the face of the gravest fear, if we are seeking to be Christ in "our world" we are not going to escape struggle and conflict.

DAY 35: INTERCESSION AS A WRESTLING MATCH

Paul closed his letter to the Ephesians with the word from the sixth chapter which was quoted at the beginning of today's reading. Then, after calling on the Ephesians to put on the whole armor of God, he begged them: "Pray at all times in the Spirit, with all prayer and supplication, to that end keep alert with all perseverance making all supplication for all the saints." (Eph. 6:18)

> In intercession we are not wrestling with God, we're wrestling for God.

Wrestling is akin to "travailing," which we discussed on Day 13, and is a good image—especially of intercessory living.

Put this understanding of intercession in the larger perspective of our relationship to God. Archbishop Richard Chenevix Trench said, "We must not conceive of prayer as an overcoming of God's reluctance, but as a laying hold of his highest willingness." In intercession we are not wrestling *with* God, we're wrestling *for* God. *Thy will be done* may be a declaration of submission in which we confess that we do not know what is best, but we want God's will. When we wrestle in prayer, however, and say, "Thy will be done," sensing there are forces in our world which are opposed to the will of God, we set ourselves against all such forces, with a raging "God's will be done, on earth, as it is in heaven."

Reflecting and Recording

1. Make some notes to describe your most recent experience of prayer as wrestling.

✣ ✣ ✣

2. In your journal briefly describe an experience in which you set yourself against forces you believed opposed the will of God.

During the Day

You are nearing the end of this intercessory journey. Find at least one person today with whom to share some of what you have experienced.

Group Meeting for Week Five

Introduction

Two disciplines are essential for meaningful group sharing: attention and intention. We must *pay attention* to what is being said, how it is being said, and we must *be intentional* about our participation.

In group settings, the easy route is laziness. Some individual group members are tempted to 'play it safe' and not risk honesty and vulnerability.

Energy is another issue. Listening and speaking demand physical and emotional energy. The temptation is to hold back, to be only half-present, and fail to invest the attention and focus essential for full participation.

I urge you to withstand those temptations and encourage you to urge fellow group members the same. Don't underestimate the value of each person's participation.

Sharing Together

1. Begin your time singing a hymn or a chorus you know by heart, i.e. "Amazing Grace," "Holy, Holy, Holy," "We're Marching to Zion," "What a Friend We Have in Jesus."
2. Invite the group to turn to 1 Peter 2:1–7, 9–10 (Day One) and read the passage together.
3. Invite three or four volunteers to share what they would say in two or three sentences if they were asked to tell what a priest is. (Reflecting and Recording, Day 29)
4. Spend a few minutes talking about how the church/community of faith of which you are a part is aware of and expresses its identity as a "chosen race," a "royal priesthood," a "holy nation," "God's own people."
5. Remind the group that a priest speaks to God *for the people* (prayer) and *to the people* for God (witness, sharing God's word). Invite two or three persons to describe how a person they know is functioning in this fashion as a priest.

6. Discuss the failure of persons in relating to others as priests, either by over-bearing or under-bearing. Urge persons to share their own experience of either failure.
7. Invite two or three people to share their experience of prayer as wrestling, or setting themselves against forces they believe opposed God's will.
8. Invite the group to spend five to ten minutes talking about an issue or issues in your community that calls for an organized prayer effort. Are there people in the group that might initiate that? Is there a prayer effort already going on that persons in the group are participating in, or might begin to do so.
9. Remind the group that they are approaching the end of this forty-day journey. You have only one other designated session, so you may want to spend some time discussing the future. Would the group like to stay together for a longer time? Are there resources (books, recordings, periodicals) the group would like to use corporately?

This book is a kind of sequel to *The Workbook of Living Prayer*, *The Workbook of Intercessory Prayer*, and *The Workbook on Abiding on Abiding in Christ*. The group may wish to choose one of those books to continue with together. Or, there may be group members, two or three individuals who would "seed" another group to use this book on The Intercessory Life, each inviting two or three to join a group to journey forty days together. People will respond more readily to you, since you have already experienced the journey. You may think of other ways to share this book with others.

Praying Together

In intercession, like the high priest bearing the tribes of Israel on his shoulder and on his heart, we can bring into God's presence persons and situations that need God's intervention. Invite persons to share their concerns. Don't wait for all concerns to be shared; as one person expresses a concern, invite a person in the group to pray for that need. Continue in this fashion until all concerns have been shared and prayed for.

As the leader closes with prayer, tell the group that next week you are going to ask each person to share the most meaningful insight they have gained, or experience they have had during this forty-day journey, and what commitment they have made for moving ahead in their Christian walk. You may think of other ways to share this book with others.

WEEK SIX

The Intercessor as Servant

DAY 36

The Downward Way

For if someone comes to you and preaches a Jesus other than the Jesus we preached, or if you receive a different spirit from the one you received, or a different gospel from the one you accepted, you put up with it easily enough. . . . I may not be a trained speaker, but I do have knowledge. We have made this perfectly clear to you in every way. . . . For such men are false apostles, deceitful workmen, masquerading as apostles of Christ. And no wonder, for Satan himself masquerades as an angel of light. It is not surprising, then, if his servants masquerade as servants of righteousness. Their end will be what their actions deserve.

—2 CORINTHIANS 11:4, 6, 13–15

ST. MARTIN WAS A FAMOUS SOLDIER-SAINT OF FRANCE. ONE DAY HE WAS PRAYING and a figure appeared to him, robed like a king with a jeweled crown and gold-embroidered shoes. A voice said to him, "Martin, recognize him whom you see. I am Christ. I am about to descend to the earth and I am showing myself to you first." A couple of minutes later, the voice went on: "Why do you hesitate, Martin, to believe me? I am Christ."

Martin replied: "The Lord Jesus did not foretell that he would come in purple and crowned in gold. I will not believe that Christ is come unless I see him in the dress and in the form in which he suffered." At that point the figure disappeared, and Martin realized it was a temptation of the devil.

Too few of us are that sensitive. Augustine wrote, "So deep has human pride sunk us that only divine humility can raise us," Augustine wrote. The signal mark of an intercessory life is humility. The primary image we have used to describe an intercessory life is priest. Our ministry as priests must be baptized in humility. So, we add to that, the image of servant as the stance of an intercessory life.

Someone described a saint as a person in whom Christ is felt to live again. I have contended throughout this study that to live the Christian life in full degree means to become 'little Christs,' which means, we live as servants.

> The signal mark of an intercessory life is humility.

This Jesus-style of servant is clearly counter-cultural. Almost from the moment we are able to pick up cues, the signals are clear: Life is a ladder and we are to climb to the top; or, it's a series of battles which we must win in order to gain the reward of success, position, money, power, influence, or prestige. In all sorts of direct and subtle ways, it is hammered into our heads that to be a real man or a real woman is not only to survive the formidable competitive struggle for success, but to be victorious. Anybody can make it to the top, we're told, if we just try harder.

The story of our Christian salvation stands radically over and against the philosophy of upward mobility. The great paradox which scripture reveals to us is that real and total freedom can be found only by *downward mobility*. The word of God came to us and lived among us as a servant. The divine way is indeed the downward way. "If any person would come after me," said Jesus, "let him deny himself, take up his cross, and follow daily" (Luke 9:23).

To be Christ in the world and live an intercessory life, then, we take our cue from Jesus himself, thus rooting ourselves in Christ, as well as in scripture.

Not only does Jesus call us to this style, he gives us life *through* this style. "Anyone who finds his life will lose it, but he who loses his life for my sake and the gospels, will find it" (Luke 9:24).

You may be thinking, *What is new about that? I've been hearing that all my life*. And you would be right. The teaching is pervasive in the recorded message of Jesus. Yet, unfortunately, that lifestyle does not characterize most Christians. I offer two signals which hopefully will cause us to consider and wrestle anew with the call of Jesus.

DAY 36: THE DOWNWARD WAY

First, being a servant is neither a matter of our own will or our own feeling, yet it incorporates both. The old George Matheson hymn is right: "My will is not my own till I have made it thine." We are given the will to be a servant. When we think that living the downward, servant way is within our reach, and that our task is simply to imitate Jesus, we have misunderstood the basic truth that is revealed to us. Modern psychology does not help us here, because it grounds human intellect and will apart from passion and desire. Too often, psychology fails to recognize that before we *will*, we *desire* and before we *act*, we *love*. The desires and loves most of us have are misplaced. This is what sin is all about. Jason Vickers expresses it clearly:

> Either we desire the wrong thing or we desire things in inappropriate ways or to an inappropriate degree. This includes our desire for food, sex, political power, and celebrity status. Even more important are the deep springs from which misplaced human desires or disordered human loves flow. If we break God's laws, then we do not do so because of a failure of the will, as though being human were primarily a matter of grit and determination. Our problem is much deeper than that.[31]

By nature, we do not have the will to be a servant. The downward servant way is God's way, not ours. The Christian life in full degree is the life in which the spirit of Christ who reaches into the depths of God is given to us by the Holy Spirit so that we may know, with a new knowledge, a new mind and a new heart, the way of God.

The second signal we need to note in the call to be a servant and live an intercessory life is this: There is a vast difference between the way most of us serve and Jesus' call to be a servant. The way most of us serve keeps us in control. We choose whom, and when, and where, and how we will serve. We stay in charge.

Jesus is calling for something else. He is calling us to be servants. And when we make this choice, we give up the right to be in charge, and that's the most difficult thing we can do.

> By nature, we do not have the will to be a servant. The downward servant way is God's way, not ours.

The most characteristic element of a servant after the style of Jesus is compassion. *Compassion* means caring with a passion. Compassion is not knowing *about* the suffering and pain of others; it is, in some way, *knowing* that pain, *entering* into it, *sharing* it, and *tasting* it, so far as possible. Why is a loved one so important to another loved one in a time of grave illness and pain? One loved one, in some mysterious way, is able to enter into the pain and the suffering of the other and be with the other at that deepest level. Though it cannot be so to that intensity and to that degree in all relationships, we are called not only to know that others, even strangers, suffer, or only to assess the painful situation in which they may be; rather, we are called to feel with the other's feelings and to act on behalf of the other.

―――――――――――――― Reflecting and Recording ――――――――――――――

1. The central thought of our reflection today is this: *The story of our Christian salvation stands radically over and against the philosophy of upward mobility. The great paradox which Scripture reveals is that real freedom can be found only in downward mobility.*

    Spend some time pondering that thought. Do you think it is true? Is it confirmed in Scripture? What other language might be used to talk about it?

    ✧ ✧ ✧

2. If *downward mobility* is the Chistian way what are some changes or on-coarse adjustments you need to make to be more Christ like. Be very clear in recording these in your journal. Make a mental note to read them about once a month for the next five or six months to see how you are following through.

    ✧ ✧ ✧

DAY 36: THE DOWNWARD WAY

During the Day

"Whoever wants to be my disciple must deny themselves and take up their cross daily and follow me. For whoever wants to save their life will lose it, but whoever loses their life for me will save it."—Luke 9:23–24

This is our memory work. Read it often today and the next few days. Commit it to memory and assess your activity by whether you are seeking to be first, or to what degree you are willing to lose your life.

DAY 37

Compassion Party on the Road

When he saw the crowds, he had compassion on them, because they were harassed and helpless, like sheep without a shepherd.

—Matthew 9:36

One of our immediate responses to the call to serve is fear . . . the fear of being manipulated, taken advantage of, used, and put in a place of weakness. Yet, amazingly, when we surrender our right to be in charge, we experience great freedom. We become available and vulnerable . . . and lose our fear in the process. When we act out of being a servant, rather than the pride producing choice to serve now and then as we please, we become bold in our compassion—and joy replaces fear.

Nothing is clearer about Jesus than the fact that he identified with and gave his life for the unblessed, the forgotten, those estranged from the system, the poor and oppressed, the suffering and the downtrodden. Spotted here and there in the gospels is a sparkling word that leaps out at us: *compassion*.

How can you and I, blessed as we are, even begin to be responsive to the needs of at least two-thirds of the world who are poor and oppressed? How can we be responsive to and care for the huge number of people in our community who live in poverty, who feel themselves unblessed, disenfranchised, oppressed? How do we enter into solidarity with those upon whom Jesus, if he returned in the flesh today, would look upon with compassion? I'm not talking only about economically poor people. I'm talking about the mentally challenged, prisoners, persons with physically handicapping conditions, the unemployed, and the unemployable. I'm talking about the elderly who are alone and are verging on helplessness, released prisoners who are seeking to reenter a straight society.

When we look at the world around us, the indwelling Christ stirs within us; our look turns into a longing, anguishing, compelling gaze of compassion and we seek ways to live out that compassion.

DAY 37: COMPASSION PARTY ON THE ROAD

I'm not doing well at it, but I'm working on it, and with penitence I beg for mercy. Though feeble in my efforts, I'm finding three expressions of solidarity and compassion that are proving meaningful and I suggest them as a channel you might explore in your own intercessory life. Hopefully, you will find some fellow servants to tackle the enterprise with you.

The first expression is *direct action*. Wherever it's possible, I must act. The Epistle of James says clearly, "if a brother or sister is ill clad and in lack of daily food and one of you says to them, 'Go in peace, be warmed and filled,' without giving them the things needed for the body, what does it profit?" (James 2:15–16 RSV). It is empty piety, and it doesn't profit anything. It is true that we are confronted and our senses are bombarded all the time with the ills of society about which we can do absolutely nothing, but when we can do something, we must.

> When we act out of being a servant, rather than the pride producing choice to serve now and then as we please, we become bold in our compassion—and joy replaces fear.

Imagine a place where people come together from different racial, economic, and cultural backgrounds to work together to grow in the gospel and overcome racism, addiction, and poverty. A church in Memphis has deliberately set out to do this. When I worshipped there recently, it was condemningly obvious: people who would never show up on Sunday morning at most Christian churches—poor, homeless, black, white, Latino, young, and old. After the service I engaged a woman in conversation. At the first opportunity she shared her testimony. She had been free from crack cocaine for eight months. I praised God with her.

It all started with a group of people, inspired by a young minister, Jamey Lee, and his wife Michelle, who moved into a poverty neighborhood, believing that their presence alone could make a witness. They had a vision of doing something. The result? Jacob's Well, opening up the doors of a church, but offering a different experience. The congregation is made up of a multicultural group of people on the fringe and those who have compassion for our city—people who are hurting throughout our city, people who have been turned off by religion, and religious people who come together for worship on Saturday evening.

Jamey says, "Those living in poverty have received handouts for years, yet the conditions in our city have only grown worse. At the same time, many enfranchised families desire to alleviate poverty in Memphis yet don't know anyone personally who is poor. Memphis is thirsty; the living water of Jacob's Well is plentiful. What better place than here? What better time than now?"

The three words that capture their mission are *reconciliation*, *rehabilitation*, and *reciprocation*. They not only worship, pray, and eat together, they *serve* together. Every Wednesday they offer CPR ("Compassion Party on the Road"). Together, the underserved and the affluent hit the streets throughout the city with sandwiches, water, and Christ as a way to reciprocate the love and mercy they have received from God. They know there are some things about which they can do nothing, but they know there are some things they can do, and they are doing it.

> Prayer is an expression of our greatest love, and it is the gateway to solidarity.

The second expression of solidarity with and compassion for others is the stewardship of money and resources. We control the way we spend our money. I make the decision as to how I use my resources of time and talent, as do you. Love expressed as compassion extends to every area of social and political concern; how we balance our personal checkbooks and order our schedules are telling markers of our Christian commitment.

The third expression of solidarity and compassion for the poor and oppressed—and this one overarches the other—is prayer, especially intercessory prayer. In a mysterious way that we may never understand, prayer is the vehicle through which we identify with, and take upon, the suffering of others. I like the way Clarence Jordan paraphrased 2 Corinthians 5:19: "God was in Christ, putting his arms around the world and hugging it to himself." Prayer is an expression of our greatest love, and it is the gateway to solidarity. Instead of keeping pain away from us, loving prayer leads us into the suffering of God for others. The deeper our love of God, the more we will suffer. The more we suffer, the more we will pray. As we embrace our suffering and the suffering of others, Christ joins us in the embrace, and our intercession becomes a channel of Christ's liberating power.

DAY 37: COMPASSION PARTY ON THE ROAD

Reflecting and Recording

Three possible expressions of solidarity and compassion are listed below. Look at your life in terms of these expressions. How you are acting or failing to act in relation to them.

- Direct Action
- Stewardship of money and resources
- Prayer

During the Day

Throughout the the day, stay open to the possibility that you may see someone, a group, or situation that if Jesus saw the same he would be "moved with compassion." Respond in whatever way you feel is appropriate in a Jesus style of serving.

DAY 38

Taking Light into Dark Places

And this is the verdict: Light has come into the world, but men loved darkness rather than light, because their deeds were evil. Everyone who does evil hates the light, and will not come into the light for fear that his deeds will be exposed. But whoever lives by the truth comes into the light, so that it may be seen plainly that what he has done has been done through God.

—John 3:19–21

GEORGE MUELLER ESTABLISHED AN "ORPHAN HOUSE" IN BRISTOL, ENGLAND, to care for orphans who would have otherwise been left helpless and homeless in an uncaring society. Mueller was convinced that God's command for his life was to do what he could to meet the need of these parentless children. His orphanage became world-famous because he was absolutely convinced that God would provide every need. He never asked for money; there was no particular church support, no fund-drives, no regular benefactors, only prayer to the God who promised to supply.

One night, Mueller's staff came to him with the bad news that there was no food in the house for breakfast the next morning, and they wanted to know what to do. Mueller told them to set the table as if all were normal and then not to worry about it. The director then went into his room, got down on his knees and poured out the need to his heavenly Father. Then he went to sleep, confident that the Lord would take care of it.

Early the next morning, a knock came on the orphanage door. It was a neighborhood baker with a load of bread and rolls. The man said that, during the night, he had gotten the feeling that the children needed some food, and the feeling was so overpowering that he simply had to go down to his shop and bake something for them. A few minutes later, another knock came on the door . . . this one from a local dairyman whose cart had broken down near the orphanage. The man knew that his milk would spoil before the cart was repaired, so he asked if the orphanage would like to have the milk.

That kind of story was repeated over and over again: George Mueller praying and God providing. Long after the "orphan house" was established and its witness known throughout the Christian world, Mueller gave this explanation as to what it was all about:

> If I, a poor man, simply by prayer and faith, obtained without asking any individual, the means for establishing and carrying on an orphan house, there would be something which, with the Lord's blessing, might be insrumental in strengthening the faith of the children of God, besides being a testimony to the consciences of the unconverted, of the reality of the things of God. This, then, was the primary reason for establishing the orphan house . . . The first and primary object of the work was (and still is) that God might be magnified by the fact that the orphans under my care are provided with all they need, only by prayer and faith without anyone being asked by me or my fellow laborers whereby it may be seen, that God is faithful still, and hears prayers still.[32]

It is easy to miss what I believe is the most important dimension of Mueller's testimony, however. The mission was to care for children, yes; but not just for the sake of caring for the children, but for "strengthening the faith of the children of God, besides being a testimony to the consciences of the unconverted, of the reality of the things of God." He wanted to demonstrate God's faithfulness.

An intercessory life is the *presence* of the reality of the things of God and demonstrates God's faithfulness. I think of that in two ways: one, taking light into dark places, and two, standing in the gap for the sake of justice and righteousness.

> An intercessory life is the *presence* of the reality of the things of God.

Jesus said, "I am . . . you are the light of the world" (John 8:12, Matt. 5:14). The place for the light is in the dark. Some of us need to confess that we would rather shine where there is light than where it is dark. It's easy to shine in the light; we are comfortable there, and there is little chance of stumbling and falling. But what difference do we make? It is in the dark that light makes its purposeful difference.

During my years as pastor of Christ United Methodist Church in Memphis, Tennessee, my wife Jerry became a volunteer chaplain in the Shelby County Jail, working with women. The job entailed some educational programs and many practical, mundane things: contacting family members, helping the inmates understand the system, interpreting rules and regulations, serving as a go-between to the jail officials and judges. It was an interecessory work: connecting, meeting, and being present as the Lord's emissary.

Jerry engaged women in our congregation to pray for the women in jail. She invited the inmates to share their concerns in writing and she would deliver those to an intercessor who would pray for that particular person. While corporate prayer was going on by all the women for the jail . . . the guards, and those who worked daily with the women and their families . . . individuals were praying for the personal concerns of a particular person.

When this had gone on for about two months, an inmate suggested they make intercession a two-way process. Why not invite the women in our congregation to share their needs and allow the inmates to pray for them? It was a powerful dynamic: upper-middle class (primarily white) women praying for and being prayed for by poor, (primarily African-American), incarcerated women.

Light was taken into a "dark place,",but now light was shining from that dark place into the "dark places" of those who presumably were "living in the light."

> Why not make intercession a two-way process?

One day Jerry said to me, "You travel to Chicago, Los Angeles, Atlanta and over the nation to preach. Why don't you come and preach to my women in the jail?" A novel idea! Why had I not thought of that? So I joined Jerry and the Christ Church praise band for many Thursday evening services. That was my first experience of jail preaching. What meaning . . . *taking light into a dark place*! And amazingly, *receiving* light out of that dark place.

Eventually, we moved from Memphis, and after being away for a year, returned to preach in the special Lenten services in downtown Calvary Episcopal Church. This series gets a lot of public attention; it is a noonday worship every weekday during the Lenten season, with visiting preachers from across the nation. I was to preach three midday services.

When Jerry and I arrived for the first, my host told me there was a woman in the parlor who had been there for an hour, waiting to greet us. We recognized her immediately. She had been in jail, had been ministered to by Jerry, had attended our worship, accepted Christ, and I had baptized her. She wanted us to know how well things were going in her life and that she was seeking to be a light in her family and community.

DAY 38: TAKING LIGHT INTO DARK PLACES

Jesus said you don't light a candle to put under a bushel, but on a candlestick, so that it will light the darkness. The purpose of a candle is not to illuminate itself but to illuminate the world. We need to remember that the darker the place, the brighter any light will shine. We must be done with the notion that in deep darkness you need something dramatic . . . a searchlight or a beacon; our praying and our intercessory presence as a simple candle can provide enough light. The size of the light and the degree of the darkness is not the issues; compassion and intentionality is.

Reflecting and Recording

1. Mueller testified that the important aspect of his mission caring for orphans without ever asking for money was to demonstrate the faithfulness of God. Think of the most powerful demonstration of the faithfulness of God that you have seen in the past few months. Make some notes to get that witness clearly in your mind.

✤ ✤ ✤

2. What in your life, in the past year, has demonstrated the faithfulness of God?

During the Day

Continue living with Luke 9:23–24 to commit it to memory and assess to what degree you are willing to lose your life, to be a servant.

DAY 39

The Go-Between for Reconciliation

Therefore, if anyone is in Christ, the new creation has come: The old has gone, the new is here! All this is from God, who reconciled us to himself through Christ and gave us the ministry of reconciliation: that God was reconciling the world to himself in Christ, not counting people's sins against them. And he has committed to us the message of reconciliation. We are therefore Christ's ambassadors, as though God were making his appeal through us. We implore you on Christ's behalf: Be reconciled to God. God made him who had no sin to be sin for us, so that in him we might become the righteousness of God."

—2 Corinthians 5:17–21

I PREACHED RECENTLY IN THE BAPTIST CHRUCH OF EAST JERUSALEM. ALEX AWAD is the pastor. His brother, Bishara, is the President of Bethlehem Bible College. They are among a forgotten people in the Middle East crisis: Palestinian Christians.

There were seven brothers and sisters in the family. The mother and father, devout Christians, taught them the ways of Christ. They were all together in the same house back in 1948. War had been raging all over the city, and now, this week, fighting was in their neighborhood and that day, on their street. At sunset the fighting died down, and their father went outside to assess what was going on.

What was going on was mindless, and sixty-five years later, it still is. Huda, the mother, heard the shot and screamed, knowing what happened, ran to her husband and dragged him into the house. Two older children helped pull the body into the dining room and lifted him onto the table. They knew immediately he was dead, caught in the crossfire between the Jordanian and Israeli armies.

The next morning, when shooting temporarily subsided, neighbors gathered in the small apartment. No priests or pastors were able to reach them. Neighborhood men had dug a grave in the courtyard behind the apartment building. Huda Awad read words of comfort from the Bible. With

DAY 39: THE GO-BETWEEN FOR RECONCILIATION

tears streaming down their faces, the children joined their mother in reciting the Lord's Prayer, and the men carried the body to the makeshift grave.

Fierce fighting resumed that afternoon, but ended before dark. In the middle of the night a Jordanian soldier came and ordered the family to evacuate because they expected the Israeli army to return any moment. "We will let you know when it is safe to return," they promised. The Awad family left and never saw their home again.

The mother got a job nursing at $25.00 per month but could not sustain the family. Bishara and Alex were placed in a home for children. Ironically, the home was next door to the building that later became the church were Alex was now the pastor and I was the guest preacher. As he told me the story, he pointed to the upstairs room where he and Bishara lived until they both, by the compassion of the Christian community, came to the U.S. to study.

Bishara and Alex are lights shining in a dark place. Both returned to their homeland, despite the violence that characterizes daily life. Bishara's first assignment was as principal of Hope Secondary School for boys located in Beit Jala, a town adjacent to Bethlehem.

He and his mother tried to visit his boyhood home, but it had been destroyed and a road built, so they couldn't find the exact location. After the 1967 war, his mother wrote to the Mayor of Jerusalem, requesting permission to move her husband's bones, but the request was ignored. So there isn't even a gravestone to mark and commerorate his father's existence.

> When we meet with God another 'meeting' can be affected.

What was not lost, however, was the gospel message and the strong Christian influence his mother and father had on Bishara. He wanted to impart that to his students. He saw that the conflict between the Israelis and Palestinians was leaving deep scars on their children. Many had lost both their parents, and many, separated from their parents during the 1967 war, did not know whether they were dead or alive. Anger and violent behaviour characterized the school community. Bishara's message which he had learned from his parents . . . love God, love your neighbor, love your enemies . . . was not getting through to his students.

"Why, Lord?" Bishara prayed. "Why are there no results? Why would you bring me back to my homeland and not use me?" Brother Andrew tells Bishara's story:

> The silence seemed to accuse him. He walked the halls past the rooms where the boys slept. Many of them tossed and turned fitfully, groaning or talking in their sleep. He wondered about their dreams, which no doubt reflected their private pains. Each of them had experienced harassment from Israeli soldiers . . . Feeling humiliated and powerless to do anything effective, many students had thrown stones at the soldiers and carried their defiance of authority over to the teachers at the school. . . .
>
> Bishara walked out the back door of the school . . . and stood under the night sky. A near full-moon illuminated Elah Valley below. This was the location where, according to many Bible experts, David had fought and defeated Goliath. In his mind Bishara could almost see the armies—the Philistines camped on the western hill, the Israelites on the east—and the nine-foot giant advancing to taunt the troops under King Saul's command. And he could see little David boldly confronting him.[33]

In a startling revelation, Bishara realized he was on the wrong side. Goliath and the Philistines verbalized the emotions he had repressed for so long. Hatred welled up in him as in his mind Goliath cursed Jesus. Bishara blamed the Israelis for the death of his father and the loss of his home in 1948, for the twelve years he had to live in an orphanage, separated from his mother, for the years of exile in the United States. The hatred had festered, but now he recognized in himself the same hatred that was in the boys under his care. As it was destroying them, it was destroying him. Unless he conquered his own anger and bitterness, he could not help them.

> Tears welled up in his eyes. How could he, a man who had given his life to Christ a dozen years before, who was committed to be an instrument of God in the Holy Land, help these young, angry boys? There was only one answer. His voice broke the silence of the night: "Lord, I beg you. Forgive me for hating the Jews and for allowing that hatred to control my life."[34]

When I shared with Bishara and his brother Alex, I knew that with every ounce of his being he had meant that prayer. The two of them are living it out as lights in the darkness. Through intercessory lives, they are providing 'meeting' (*paga*), demonstrating that when we meet with God another 'meeting' can be affected. We meet with God, asking him to meet with someone else and we become the go-between (another meaning for intercession) that brings reconciliation.

Bishara and Alex may not be thinking this way, but they are demonstrating that intercession is not primarily a prayer a person prays, but something a person does. Through their intercessory lives they are providing "meeting" (*paga*) for Palestinian Christian, Arab Muslims, Jews, and Messianic

DAY 39: THE GO-BETWEEN FOR RECONCILIATION

Jews. It is a slow, frustrating, painful process, but now and then reconciliation happens and light shines in the darkness.

I have missed the mark if a dramatic story like this blinds you to the opportunities for intercession (meeting) in what you may think is a prosaic life. You can prayer walk in your neighborhood, asking God to meet with families and save them, guide them, comfort them. You can pray for guidance and talk with friends about the most neglected and underserved people in your community . . . how might you reach out to them and provide meeting? If you live in an urban area, there are immigrants who need a sign of God's love and care; you can be that sign simply by expressing concern and being present to them. In small towns and rural areas, there are people who are "outsiders." They are looked down on because they receive food stamps and government assistance; they have not been fortunate to get an education and they feel they have no place to belong . . . not even in church. By intentional expressions of compassion you can be the light in dark places.

> By intentional expressions of compassion you can be the light in dark places.

Reflecting and Recording

1. In your journal, name some of the people in your church and/or community who are shining light in dark places. Describe their lives and what they are doing.

✤ ✤ ✤

2. Recall an occasion when you could have shined a light but failed to do so. Make enough notes to get the experience in your mind.

✤ ✤ ✤

3. Live with that experience of failure prayerfully for a few minutes. What did you learn from that experience? Are you willing to make a commitment now that you will seek to live an intercessory life, that you will seek to be light and practice the ministry reconciliation?

✤ ✤ ✤

During the Day

Seek specific occasions for the expression of your commitment.

DAY 40

Standing in the Gap

I looked for a man among them who would build up the wall and stand before me in the gap on behalf of the land so I would not have to destroy it, but I found none.

—Ezekiel 22:30

It's difficult to talk about light in the fashion we have considered without recalling the song we loved as children and which some of us adults still like to sing: "This Little Light of Mine."

Children love the second verse most: "Hide it under a bushel? No! I'm gonna let it shine . . . "

But we do, don't we? Even in the church. In fact, the church is sometimes the bushel under which we hide the light. We hide the light when we restrict its glow inside church walls for a few hours a week. We hide the light when we refuse to confront human sinfulness; we hide the light when we fail to challenge culture's sins and bondage to racism and sexism. We hide the light when we order our lives and the life of the church, giving in to the materialism and consumerism of our day. Most of all, we hide it when we ourselves, as Christ followers, are not on fire with intercessory zeal, knowing that "God did not give us a spirit of timidity, but a spirit of power, of love and of self-discipline" (2 Tim. 1:7).

But not only do we take our light into dark places, living an intercessory life, *we stand in the gap for the sake of justice and righteousness.*

That is what Alex and Bishara, about whom we shared yesterday, are doing in Bethlehem and Jerusalem. They are shining a light in dark places and standing in the gap for the sake of justice and righteousness.

The image of 'standing in the gap' comes from the prophet Ezekiel.

Along with all the prophets, Ezekiel constantly confronted God's people about their failure to be holy and righteous, to sustain their integrity as the "people of God." When young, Ezekiel was among those deported from Jerusalem to Babylon, he witnessed the life of his exiled people and, in a vision, saw his nation finally destroyed, and even to his horror, the holy city and the temple reduced to ruins.

He called individuals and the nation to fulfill the covenant requirements and he warned them of the inevitable results of refusing to do so. God's people were called to be "holy, as God was holy." In the first verses of chapter 22, he gives dramatic expression to how Israel and her leaders have failed:

> See how each of the princes of Israel who are in you uses his power to shed blood. In you they have treated father and mother with contempt; in you they have oppressed the alien and mistreated the fatherless and the widow. You have despised my holy things and desecrated my Sabbaths. In you are slanderous men bent on shedding blood; in you are those who eat at the mountain shrines and commit lewd acts. In you are those who dishonor their fathers' bed; in you are those who violate women during their period, when they are ceremonially unclean. In you one man commits a detestable offense with his neighbor's wife, another shamefully defiles his daughter-in-law, and another violates his sister, his own father's daughter. In you men accept bribes to shed blood; you take usury and excessive interest and make unjust gain from your neighbors by extortion. And you have forgotten me, declares the Sovereign Lord.—Ezekiel 22:6–12

All the Ten Commandments, broken; total violation of concerns about holy living. Ezekiel concludes his prophetic blast with a sad word from God, which is also a word of judgment: "I looked for a man among them who would build up the wall and stand before me in the gap on behalf of the land so I would not have to destroy it, but I found none" (v. 30).

Ezekiel used the image of a watchman. In his day, the Jews had the custom of building watchtowers in their fields and vineyards for a person to keep watch at harvest time to warn of approaching hostile people coming to steal the harvest. Ezekiel was keenly aware that God had called him to be a watchman, a messenger to warn the Israelites of the impending destruction for those who did not give up their evil ways. Is it too much of a stretch to think that living an intercessory life carries that same responsibility? Certainly the corporate body of intercessors, the church, must speak and live in a way to warn people of the consequences of sin, and the danger of living in violation of God's justice and righteousness.

Early in his book, Ezekiel makes it clear that not only is he, as a watchman, to be faithful in warning the people, if he failed to do so, he would be held responsible. Just as God made Ezekiel responsible, God makes those who give themselves to standing in the gap in intercession responsible and holds them accountable.

It was dramatic with Ezekiel; if he allowed the wicked to die unwarned, God threatened to require their lives at the prophet's own hand. God says to him, "Therefore groan, son of man! Groan before them with broken heart and bitter grief" (Ezek. 21:6).

Here is the dynamic of speaking to the people for God and speaking to God for the people by groaning. It is both prophetic and priestly action: intervention and intercession.

> To stand in the gap and take light into the darkness often requires struggle and emotional pain.

To stand in the gap and take light into the darkness often requires struggle and emotional pain. We identify with and we want to intervene, though often there is no sign of appreciation or receptivity. In fact, there are many occasions when we are rebuffed, even scorned. But we continue to 'groan' before them with broken heart and bitter grief.

I have come to believe that the grace of God is so radical that, when we express it in its fullness, we may be thought to accept the sins and the lifestyle of the people we seek to serve. With that thought in mind, the measure of our intercession may be indicated by response to these questions.

Who are the people in your community who have yet to receive a clear message from you personally, and from the church, that you deeply care for them and that God loves them?

What about the growing population of those in recovery—those seeking freedom from alcohol and drugs? Are you and your community of faith a place of welcome and hospitality that will help them break the chains of shame and blame?

What about the sexually broken? Is the only message they hear a word of condemnation that comes from those who lambast them with passages of cold truth from scripture? Are you groaning with those who struggle with their sexual identity and those who use their bodies for money to feed their family?

What about the poor? Are we speaking to our people for God who, if he loves one people more than any other, it is the poor? What about the working poor, chief among them single mothers?

"Son of Man, groan!" God said to Ezekiel, and he says to us. Show the people that you care, that you speak for a God who loves us, who forgives our iniquities and heals our diseases, who restores us to wholeness and gives us joy, and to whom we are making intercession on their behalf.

Dutch Sheets has provided a very helpful insight about our taking the light into the darkness and standing in the gap. He says responsibility in intercession is to "enforce the victory as we also meet the powers of darkness." He makes this statement in the context of Christ's victory over Satan and the powers of darkness. We are to enforce the victory that has already been won. On the cross, Jesus shouted "*Tetelestai,*" the Greek word for "It is finished," in John 19:30. Jesus was not speaking about death. *Tetelestai* means to fully accomplish something, or bring it to its completed state. Sheets reminds us that the word was also stamped on invoices in that day meaning, "Paid in full."

This was Jesus' intercession for us. We, through our prayers and our intercessory life, meet the powers of darkness, enforcing the victory Christ accomplished when He met them in his work of intercession.

The intercessor is either going to *meet* with God for the purpose of reconciling the world to the Father and His wonderful blessings, or he is going to *meet* Satanic forces of opposition—and at times, maybe both—to enforce the victory already won.[35]

That brings me back to "This Little Light of Mine." The third verse says, "Won't let Satan blow it out." I like that, and I especially like the spirit children express when they sing it. "Won't let Satan blow it out. *Puff.* I'm gonna let it shine." But there is a problem with it.

> We are to enforce the victory that has already been won.

Dare we even think Satan can blow our light out? To be sure, we must be vigilant in our "shining" and in cultivating the "light." But again, our intercession is to enforce the victory already won as we confront the powers of darkness. The powers of sin and death have already been destroyed. Let Satan try to blow it out, let the powers of darkness have their best shot—we can trust the light of Christ which shines in us. That light "shines in the darkness and the darkness has never put it out" (John 1:5). We don't need to think about preserving or protecting the light. An intercessory life will light other "candles" and more dark places will be invaded and illumined.

DAY 40: STANDING IN THE GAP

---— Reflecting and Recording ———

1. Reflect on your forty-day journey. Make some notes about what you have experienced . . . lessons learned, fresh insight about old ideas, questions you have, relationships you have established, and decisions you have made.

✤ ✤ ✤

2. Spend a bit of time thinking about how you might describe this forty-day journey to another person.

✤ ✤ ✤

3. If you are a part of a group, today may be your last scheduled gathering. What do you want to share with the group? Is there some way you might want the group to continue together? Is there some corporate action you would like the group to engage in?

✤ ✤ ✤

---— During the Day ———

For a season, possibly three or four weeks, begin each day saying to yourself, *THIS DAY, I WILL LIVE AN INTERCESSORY LIFE.*

Closing Group Meeting And Celebration

Introduction

Last week, you may have discussed whether your group wants to continue meeting. Here are possibilities to consider.

- Select two or three weeks of this book that were especially challenging or meaningful. Repeat those weeks in more depth to extend your time together.
- Decide to continue meeting as a group, using another resource. I noted possibilities for this in keeping with the kind of experience you have had with this forty-day journey: *The Workbook of Living Prayer*, *The Workbook of Intercessory Prayer*, and *The Workbook on Abiding in Christ*.
- If you wish to go in that direction, you should select the resource now and ask a person to secure the books, get them to the persons who wish to participate and set a time for your first meeting.

It is very probable that many people within your church or the faith community are looking for a small-group experience, so one or two persons in this group may decide to recruit and lead another group through *The Intercessory Life*.

Sharing Together

Facilitator: save at least thirty minutes for the last discussion point, and ten minutes for closing prayer and celebration.

1. Spend a few minutes talking about the claim that there is a vast difference between the way most of us serve and Jesus' call to be a servant.

2. If it is true that downward mobility is the way to real freedom in our Christian faith and way, how do we put that dynamic into action?
3. Spend ten to fifteen minutes discussing taking light into dark places and standing in the gap as primary expressions of an intercessory life. Tell stories of persons you know who are doing that and how they are doing it.
4. Last week you were asked to come prepared to share the most meaningful insight you have gained, or experience you have had during this forty-day journey, and what commitment you have made for moving ahead in your Christian walk. Spend the balance of your sharing time doing that. Persons may share more than once, but make sure every person has the opportunity to share.

Praying Together

In your closing prayer time, stand in a circle and sing together "This Little Light of Mine." Urge persons who might have used motions singing the song in the past to feel free to add motions. Let this be a joyful celebration.

Now, invite people to hold hands in a circle and share any word of need, concern, celebration, or joy; then have a prayer time, involving as many people as are willing to offer prayers . . . of thanksgiving for the experience; intercession for persons or concerns that have been shared; and for the churches that are represented in the group, as well as petitions for further growth and guidance.

When the leader senses that all have prayed who wish to do so, invite the group to join in praying the Lord's Prayer.

Endnotes And Works Cited

1. John Flavel, *The Works of John Flavel*, Vol. 5 (Carlisle: Banner of Truth, 1968 [1820]), 424, 428.
2. A.W. Tozer, *The Pursuit of God* (Camp Hill, Pa.: Wing Spread Publications, 1993), 23.
3. Brennan Manning, *Posers, Fakers and Wannabes* (Colorado Springs: NavPress, 2003), 10.
4. Maxie Dunnam, *The Workbook of Intercessory Prayer* (Nashville: The Upper Room, 1979), 7–8).
5. Maxie Dunnam, *The Workbook of Living Prayer* (Nashville: The Upper Room, 1994), 69.
6. Ibid., 72.
7. Andrew Murray, *The Ministry of Intercession* (New Kensington: Whitaker House, 2001), 151.
8. Jack Hayford, *Prayer Is Invading the Impossible* (South Plainville, H.Y.: Logos International, 1977; revised edition, Bridge Publishing, 1995, p. 92, l977 edition)
9. Maxie Dunnam, *The Workbook of Abiding in Christ* (Nashville: The Upper Room, 2010), 129.
10. F.B. Meyer, *Devotional Commentary on Exodus* (Grand Rapids: Kregel Publications, l978), 444–445.
11. Lloyd Olgilvie, *The Communicator's Commentary, Vol. 5, Acts* (Waco: Word Books, 1983), 23.
12. Dutch Sheets, *Intercessory Prayer* (Ventura: Regal Books, 1996), 123.
13. John Baillie, *Christian Devotion* (London: Oxford University Press, 1962), 26.
14. Maxie Dunnam, *Lessons From the Saints* (Nashville: The Upper Room Books, 2002), 77.
15. Hudson Taylor, quoted in Howard Taylor and Geraldine Taylor, *Hudson Taylor's Spiritual Secret* (Chicago: Moody Press, 1955), 153.
16. Ibid., 56.
17. Ibid., l63.
18. *Mere Christianity*, quoted by Foster, Devotional Classics, p.10
19. Samuel Chadwick, *The Way to Pentecost* (Fort Washington: Christian Literature Crusade, 1969), 15.
20. David Miller, *The Lord of Bellavista* (Nappanee: Evangel Publishing House,1999).
21. Marcus Dods, *How to Become Like Christ* (Gutenberg EBook, 2006), 8–9.
22. *A Year with the Saints,* (Rockford, Ill.: Tan Book and Publishers, Inc., 1891), 227.
23. Maxie Dunnam, *The Communicators Commentary, Vol. 8* (Waco: Word Books, 1982), 361.
24. Ibid., 67.
25. Alexander MacLaren, *Expositions of Holy Scripture, Vol. 11* (Ada: Baker Book House, 1982), 312.
26. See Dutch Sheets, *Intercessory Prayer*, for an excellent discussion of intercessors meeting with God and meeting with the powers of darkness, pp. 50ff.
27. F.B. Meyer, *Studies in Exodus* (Grand Rapids: Kregel Publications,1978), 358.
28. Dutch Sheets, *Intercessory Prayer* (Ventura: Regal Books, 1996), 219.
29. F.B. Meyer, *Studies in Exodus* (Grand Rapids: Kregel Publications,1978), 361.
30. L. Ellsworth Kalas, "Prayer: Sometimes I Wrestle,",a sermon preached at Church of the Savior, Cleveland, Ohio, May 5, 1985.
31. Jason Vickers, *Minding the Good Ground* (Waco: Baylor University Press, 2011), 6l.
32. George Mueller, *Answers to Prayer*, comp. A. E. C. Brooks (Chicago: Moody, n. d.) 9–10, quoted by David Platt, *Radical*, (Colorado Springs: Multnomah Press, 2010) 55.
33. Brother Andrew, *Light Force* (London: Hodder & Stoughton, 2004), 103.
34. Ibid., 104.
35. Dutch Sheets, *Intercessory Prayer* (Ventura: Regal Books, 1996), 55–58.

About the Author

Dr. Maxie Dunnam became the fifth president of Asbury Theological Seminary in 1994. After serving ten years as president, Dr. Dunnam became chancellor for four years before retiring in 2008. During Dr. Dunnam's presidency of Asbury Seminary, the school pioneered the use of technology, establishing a virtual campus and also founding a second geographical campus in Orlando, Florida.

Prior to his presidency at Asbury, Dunnam served twelve fruitful years as Senior Minister of Christ United Methodist Church, a 6,000-member congregation in Memphis, Tennessee. His tenure at Christ Church was marked by a commitment to evangelism, inner-city ministries, housing for the working poor, outreach to the recovering community, and innovative worship. His provocative one-minute radio and television message, *Perceptions*, is being replicated all over the nation.

He came to Christ Church from serving as World Editor of *The Upper Room*. During his service at *The Upper Room*, the Walk to Emmaus and the Academy of Spiritual Formation were begun.

He is as active now as ever, mentoring young ministers and serving on the staff of Christ UMC as Director of Christ Church Global. His current mission focus in Memphis is public education, (believing that public education is the civil rights issue of the twenty-first century) and planting faith communities among the underserved.

Dr. Dunnam is a powerful and prolific writer, having authored more than forty books, including *The Workbook of Living Prayer,* which sold over one million copies.